Praise for
Falling for God

"Gary Moon writes with a combination of thoughtfulness, guidance, and joy that will serve every reader. He has taken the deepest longing of the soul and the wisdom of great minds from past centuries and woven them in a way that is accessible and helpful to any who want to grow close to God."

— JOHN ORTBERG, teaching pastor of Menlo Park Presbyterian Church, Menlo Park, California, and author of *Everybody's Normal Till You Get to Know Them*

"Gary's use of story, imagery, and an uncommon vocabulary masterfully stir our heart's hunger for God himself. He also gives us practical ways to revel in the love of our ever-pursuing God. He has encouraged me to listen anew to the voice of my Father."

—DIANE LANGBERG, PH.D., psychologist and author of *Counseling Survivors of Sexual Abuse* and *On the Threshold of Hope*

"Not many books stir hope that my appetite for God can actually be satisfied in this crazy, disappointing world. *Falling for God* does. In these well-written pages, Gary offers profound, simple, practical, and warm companionship on the journey that matters most."

—LARRY CRABB, speaker, psychologist, author of *The Pressure's Off,* and founder of New Way Ministries

"With heart-stopping insights, practical suggestions, and sly wit, Gary Moon draws readers toward Christ so powerfully that we long to bow our hearts in worship. *Falling for God* is destined to become a classic on spiritual formation."

—SANDRA D. WILSON, PH.D., seminary professor and author of *Into Abba's Arms*

"Who could resist falling for God when Christian spirituality is properly understood as a love affair of cosmic proportions! If your heart longs for Perfect Love, this book is for you. It speaks to head, heart, and body, as all are involved in the transforming romance that God offers."

—DAVID G. BENNER, PH.D., C.PSYCH., distinguished professor of psychology and spirituality, Psychological Studies Institute in Atlanta

"Replete with relevant Bible studies and personal meditations, this book points us, among other things, to spiritual exercises that have been the mainstay of many of God's saints for a long time. Author Gary Moon helps us open up our conversations with God, teaching us the art of listening to, not just talking with, him. We are drawn into a deep hunger for God as a desire to live with him at the center of our being is fostered."

—ARCHIBALD D. HART, PH.D., FPPR, senior professor of psychology and dean emeritus, Graduate School of Psychology, Fuller Theological Seminary

"This new book from the pen of Gary Moon is a magnificent contribution to men and women in search of God's love at the deepest parts of their inner being. Gary knows precisely what it takes to form a great life, and it all starts with a highly intimate sense of who God is and how he feels about you. I am convinced that following the principles in this book can change a reader's life from drab to scintillating."

—NEIL CLARK WARREN, PH.D., author of *Finding the Love of Your Life* and founder of eHarmony.com

Falling for God

Falling for God

Saying Yes
to His Extravagant Proposal

Gary W. Moon

SHAW BOOKS

an imprint of WATERBROOK PRESS

Falling for God
A SHAW BOOK
PUBLISHED BY WATERBROOK PRESS
2375 Telstar Drive, Suite 160
Colorado Springs, Colorado 80920
A division of Random House, Inc.

Portions of "Plato's Cave" in chapter 2, "Becoming Open to Love," appeared in a different version in *Homesick for Eden* by Gary Moon, copyright © 1997, published by Servant Publications. Portions of the story about Regina in the conclusion, "Say Yes to God's Extravagant Proposal," appeared in a different version in *Homesick for Eden* by Gary Moon, copyright © 1997, published by Servant Publications. Portions of the introduction, "Misplaced Passions," appeared in a slightly different version in *Conversations: A Forum for Authentic Transformation*, Spring 2003, 48-50. Portions of "Dancin' Boy" in chapter 2, "Becoming Open to Love," appeared in a slightly different version in *Conversations: A Forum for Authentic Transformation,* Spring 2003, 71-2.

ISBN 0-87788-076-X

Library of Congress Cataloging-in-Publication Data
Moon, Gary W., 1956–
    Falling for God : saying yes to his extravagant proposal / by Gary W. Moon.
      p. cm.
Includes bibliographical references.
    ISBN 0-87788-076-X
  1. Spiritual life—Christianity. I. Title.
    BV4501.3.M65 2004
    248.4—dc22

                                                2003021756

Printed in the United States of America
2004—First Edition

10 9 8 7 6 5 4 3 2 1

Contents

Foreword by Dallas Willard ix

Acknowledgments xi

Introduction: *Misplaced Passions* 1

1 The Three Cs of Lasting Love 7
   Conversation, Communion, and Consummation

Part 1: Conversation
Talking to God Without Losing Your Mind

2 Becoming Open to Love 29
   Understanding the Kingdom of God
3 Deciding to "Go Steady" 47
   Practicing the Presence of God
4 Learning to Listen 68
   How to Hear God's Voice

Hanging Out with God—All the Time 89
   Frank Laubach

Part 2: Communion
It's Not Just for Sunday Anymore

5 Saying Yes to Fidelity 95
   Turning Away from Other Loves

6 Fear of Total Commitment 112
      How Communion Exposes My False Self

7 Surrender Hurts 131
      The Sweet Ache of Letting Go

Living Out of the Divine Center 149
      Thomas R. Kelly

Part 3: Consummation
Christ Incarnate in Me

8 Forgiveness 155
      The Importance of Staying Connected to Love

9 Reconciliation 173
      Awakening to the Desire to Be United with God Forever

10 Union with God 190
      Less of Me, More of Him

One Woman's Pursuit of Union with God 209
      Teresa of Avila

Conclusion: *Say Yes to God's Extravagant Proposal* 212

Notes 219

Foreword

This book is about life lived in constant, close contact with God, a life in which "Look, I am always with you"—as said by Jesus to his friends—becomes a day-to-day reality. It is about real life lived now in the kingdom of heaven.

Such a life will never be imposed upon us, nor will it occur automatically. It doesn't just happen to us, no matter how many wonderful church services we may attend. Though it is a gift, it does not come to those who are passive. It comes only in response to intelligent, informed, purposive, sustained, and interactive relationship with Jesus now living in our world. That is why we are directed to "grow in the grace and knowledge of our Lord and Savior Jesus Christ" (2 Peter 3:18). Persistent, strenuous, and well-directed action is required.

To that end, we need *information:* specific, down-to-earth directions on what to do. We need *imagination:* pictures and stories of what we will encounter along the path of growing to know Jesus better. We need *persistence:* the will to consistently stick to and apply the means to our goal. We need *patience:* a willingness to let the life we are living grow and take the wise course. And we need *realism:* a clear eye and a confidence that it's safe and necessary to call things by their true name.

These attributes are not readily come by in our world or in our religious circles. Images of "success" all around us run in the opposite direction. American religious history and practice is tied to a revivalist tradition, full of magic figures and magic moments. How many announcements and advertisements have you recently heard that promise "life-changing" or "life-transforming" services or programs? If a significant portion of these actually came true, we would by now have nothing for policemen to do.

As a result, many people cease to believe that life can be transformed, that we really can put off the old person and put on the new person, which is the character of Christ. They settle for a life that is no different from that of other "good people," plus heaven when they die. Or they throw over the whole project of Christlikeness, possibly allowing it may be for some people but not for them.

Here this book can help. Rich in biblical and psychological understanding, it brings the dearest treasures of the Christian spiritual life within reach of the serious contemporary apprentice of Jesus in kingdom living. You will have to sit with it, stew in it—in short make it a priority and a project. ("Seek *first* the his kingdom and his righteousness," you may recall.) (Matthew 6:33). But if you do, you will certainly come to know what it means to grow—steadily, reliably—in grace. Grace is actually God acting in our lives to accomplish, with our participation, what we cannot accomplish on our own. This is eternal life now, a life of interactive relationship that leaves neither the here nor the hereafter in doubt.

Falling for God is charmingly honest and rich in content and illustrations. Gary Moon sees into the soul and then deftly shows how to unsnarl the lines of communication and influence that open us up to God. His gentle and humorous style will hold you close but convey the deepest spiritual lessons at the same time. He shows us that the best way to become like Jesus and be at home in his kingdom is by entering into a journey with him, a transformational excursion of conversation, communion, and consummation.

—DALLAS WILLARD

Acknowledgments

Liz Heaney is an amazing editor! Even though I had written several books prior to this one, I had never been seriously edited. There's a better way to say that. My prior experience with editing had been like going to the dentist to get my teeth cleaned. It was a valuable experience. But working with you, Liz, has been more like being treated by an orthodontist—and getting a root canal while you wait. And sometimes you didn't use enough Novocain. But the thing is, I really like my new smile.

Liz, thank you. You are truly gifted. While I don't want to even think about another office visit—for at least a year—I never want to write again unless you would be willing to do all the extracting and straightening.

I'm also very grateful to the folks at my day jobs. To Jeff Terrell, president of the Psychological Studies Institute, and Greg Hearn, CEO of LifeSprings Resources, thanks for letting me slow down the pace of teaching and writing a bit so I could complete this project. I hope this free plug makes us even.

Finally, I am eternally grateful to Regina, my wife, and Jesse and Jenna, my two daughters. You have all been so patient with the laborious process of making a book, a husband, and a father. Thank you.

Oh, and Mom, don't forget that for you to buy one hundred copies was part of the contract.

Misplaced Passions

As I sit down to write this book, a question that has been waving for my attention for more than two decades races to center stage and grabs the microphone: If Jesus came to turn our world right-side up, why do so many of his followers continue to live such upside-down lives? Why do I?

If Jesus came to our planet so that all who would listen could be restored to relationship with the Father and enjoy the heavenly emotions of love, joy, and peace, why do Christians commonly feel as if we are alone in the world and burdened by the earthbound feelings of anger, depression, and anxiety?

Do you ever feel that no matter how hard you try or how much you desire it, the bountiful life Jesus promised continues to elude you? If you do, the solution may not be as simple as ducking into the nearest church for assistance. In the words of Dallas Willard, the Christian church does not provide a coherent curriculum for finding and experiencing abundant life. If it did, church growth consultants and psychologists would have gone the way of telegraph operators. Yet both vocations are booming, as indispensable as e-mail.

But why? Why do so few Christians actually enjoy and celebrate the good news—the abundant life promised by Jesus? Why is it only the saints who have taken Christianity 101? Or in the words of one of Walker Percy's characters in *The Second Coming,* "If the good news is true, why is no one pleased to hear it?"

I'll cut to the chase. *I believe that ninety-nine out of a hundred Christians rarely enjoy the rich life that Christ promised; they live, instead, lives of silent resignation.* If you are with the one, slide this book back on the shelf. You don't need it. But if you are like me, among the ninety-nine, then this book is for

1

you. Together we're going to explore how we can enter into a process of spiritual formation that will result in the forming of the life and character of Christ within the heart. It's all about being willing to fall in love.

A REAL STORY

For a number of months, while practicing as a psychologist, I met weekly with a young man in his early thirties. He was painfully shy and tormented by anxiety. More than anything in the world, Dave wanted to find a wife. He dreamed of being with a special person for conversation, communion, and union.

Dave's relationship history was almost a blank page. Except for writing about the pain of rejection, it was.

He had been turned down for dates so many times he eventually quit asking. It had been seventeen years since he had gotten his driver's license—an event he fantasized would signal more dating opportunities—but he'd only experienced a woman (other than his mother) sitting in the passenger seat two times. Neither had said yes to a second outing.

Not long before Dave began meeting with me, a "friend" of his had suggested that he satisfy his need for company with the opposite sex by going to a bar where scantily clad women would bring him a drink, and, for additional money, would become even scantier before his eyes.

Dave was hooked after one visit and became a regular. Money was not a problem for him. Intimacy was the problem, and it became easy for him to confuse the presence of a woman, meaningless banter, and seminudity with relationship.

Here's the truly unsettling thing. I believe Dave's experiences bear a remarkable similarity to the way many Christians relate to God, which may explain why so many of us become dissatisfied with our relationship with him. We attend church at about the same frequency Dave was visiting bars. We've enjoyed brief encounters with God and have had moments of spiritual excitement. But these experiences have never led to a real relationship of meaningful conversation, intimate communion, or union. Like Dave, we have experienced flirtation but not fact, words but not dialogue, promises but not commitment, and ultimately, distance instead of communion. Given our approach, union with God is less likely than getting a good snow cone in hell.

I hope I've not offended you, but I believe this image is very important. I believe it captures how many of us do church—momentary encounters with God instead of the development of a deep and lasting relationship with someone we can take home to meet Mom. Christian spiritual formation and the experience of abundant living can only happen as we fall head over heels in love with God.

GOD'S ABSURD INVITATION

God has offered us an incredible invitation to enter into intimate relationship with himself. Relationship. Loving connection with the One who sketched out the first atom, hung the stars without string, and crafted your soul with greater love than your mom felt as she knitted your first booties. Connection with the One who loves you with the romantic love of a groom for his bride.

Romantic? Yes. God's desire for love is stronger than your own, and his use of loving imagery in describing it is enough to make a bartender blush. The foreshadowing backdrop to Jesus' first miracle is a week-long wedding celebration in Cana. He leaves his apprentices with the charge to become one with the Father, and he calls the church his bride and himself the Groom. A bride invited to be at the greatest wedding celebration in the history of the universe, the Marriage Supper of the Lamb.[1]

It boggles the mind. Why would God want to develop a loving relationship with me? What do I have to offer him that he doesn't already have at 10^{40}? What's in it for him? This can't be right! Even my spouse and kids need a break from being with me. Could the Creator of heaven and earth really desire to be my friend? my lover? closer than newlyweds on their honeymoon night? And forever and ever? Wow!

It's difficult for me to wrap my brain around the fact that I am not just saved *from* but *to,* that I'm saved to restored intimacy with God. With salvation comes an invitation to join in with the Trinity as part of their eternal community of love. And with it the offer to enjoy intimate fellowship that surpasses what is possible in the best of marriages.

But it is far too easy to become distracted from our journey into intimacy with God. Sometimes heady questions get in the way. What would Jesus do? or eat? or think? Would Jesus buy an Oldsmobile or a Toyota? Would he drink Pepsi or wine? Would he think about politics or religion? Who knows? Are these the questions we should be asking? I don't think so, because they allow us to appreciate Jesus from a distance, or as a belief system, instead of as a live-in, twenty-four-hour-a-day intimate friend.

The better question, the real question, is: How will I *be* as Jesus lives his life through me? Jesus, not sitting on a throne in heaven, but here with me in the muck and mire of life, here with me as an intimate companion—incarnate once again, but this time *in* me as the lover of my soul, who never leaves to go to the mall or to watch a football game.

With this staggering possibility, however, comes a sobering observation. Most marriages to Christ never get consummated. Most never experience the joy of union. Why? I believe it's because we fail to pursue him with the same reckless abandon with which we chased (or will chase) our spouse. We settle for brief encounters instead of intimate dialogue and become content with the contract instead of enjoying communion. Or perhaps the notion of viewing God in a romantic way frightens us, as does the possibility of losing the boundary of our self in the ocean of his love.

I pray this book creates in you a desire and willingness to take the time to fall hopelessly in love with God, so that you might experience the union you were created to enjoy.

GETTING THE MOST FROM THIS BOOK

What's the big idea behind this book? It's simply this: Restoration of the soul—change that leads to abundant life in Christ and the emotions of love, joy, and peace—happens as we cultivate a passionate relationship with God. So this is a romance novel of sorts, but without the wind-blown couple on the cover.

In the pages that follow I attempt to explore what it means to fall head over heels in love with God and to offer a potpourri of practical suggestions for how we can invite God to make real changes in our lives through the experience of his love. So you won't just think I'm a hopeless idealist, at the end of the three sections, I introduce you to a person who did what we are talking about in this book. Because these three people fell head over heels in love with God, their lives were incredibly transformed.

I wrote this book with the hope that it can be experienced at different levels and different speeds. Each chapter presents a particular theme of spiritual formation relevant to growing an ever-deepening relationship with God. If you are looking for a story-filled, curl-up-by-the-fireplace book, I think you'll find that here.

If you want to slow down and experience this book, I've included some exercises at the end of each chapter that target your head, heart, body, and soul.

- *For Your Head—A Bible Study.* At the conclusion of each chapter you will find a Bible study that will take you to Scripture for the purpose of delving more deeply into the chapter theme. These studies can be used for either private devotion or small group study.
- *For Your Heart—Personal Meditations.* These reflections on the chapter themes will prompt interaction with the historic model of transformation, which includes: *purgation* (releasing our hold on the world), *illumination* (growing realization of the power and presence of God), and *union* (a growing experiential understanding of the mystery of "Christ-in-me").

5

- *For Body and Soul—Classic Spiritual Exercises.* One or more classic spiritual exercises intended to help you experience the Christian formation theme presented in the chapter.

If you do these activities, they can provide you with a deeper experience of the material covered in the chapter. Or you may simply think of them as suggestions of what to do on a date with God.

Enough introducing. Let's turn our attention to the three Cs of a lasting love with God—*conversation, communion, and consummation.* As you journey toward union, don't be surprised if the world begins to look right-side up.

Chapter 1

The Three Cs of Lasting Love

Conversation, Communion, and Consummation

> *We were made to live in his perfect love, we were meant to walk in his grace. And we'll never feel we are home again until we see him face to face.*

CLAIRE CLONINGER

As surely as a fish is designed to feel at home in water, you were crafted for a particular environment. You were uniquely designed to be at home in the ocean of God's love. Your soul was made for connection to God and others. Somewhere deep inside, you know that, and perhaps sometimes you feel a twinge of homesickness for the life God created you to have.

We don't have to flip through many pages of Scripture before bumping into the fact that each of us is very special to God. He made us in his own image. Because he is a community of compassion, love is our natural habitat. He wired us to feel at home in a place like the Garden of Eden, which literally means "pleasure" or "delight." He programmed each of us for intimate connection.

Adam and Eve fell from grace and into an unnatural habitat, like fish trying to swim in a forest. If we listen in silence, we can almost hear their cry as it echoes through time. (Or is it coming from our own hearts?) Nothing awakens the deepest feelings of terror like the experience of separation from love.

Ever since the Fall, every human heart has experienced a longing to go home, to live in love with God and one another. Jesus knew that. He came to earth with the wonderful news that God invites us to come home. He has opened wide the gate to Eden. He's banished the guards, freshly manicured the grounds, kicked out the snakes.

Jesus referred to our garden home as "the kingdom." He told everyone that the laws that govern the land are pure and simple: Live in love with God and one another until your heart beats as one with the Trinity.

Yes, you have been invited back home and to a wedding. To your home. To your wedding. But it won't be a shotgun affair. God has been very patient in his love through the milleniums. He knows that it will take some time to get to know him and for trust to be earned. He knows that we will need to develop our relationship with him the same way all romantic relationships progress.

While our journey begins with salvation, we will fall deeply in love with God as we get to know him through taking the time for *conversation,* becoming honest enough for true *communion,* and ultimately, trusting his desire for *consummation* and surrendering to it. The road that goes back home stops at a wedding chapel.

Why is this important? Because most of us don't take the time to walk this less-traveled road, the path of true intimacy, oneness, and union in our relationship with God. Most do not realize that these three Cs—conversation, communion, and consummation—are the only route that leads to soul transformation and the experience of life in full.

Transforming Conversation Requires Time

I think you would've liked Howard and Nellie—my wife's grandparents. They fell in love as teenagers in the mountains of western Virginia, and they stayed that way for more than sixty years.

Howard was a barber. He cut hair and shaved faces at a little shop on Main Street nestled between a soda joint with marble counters and the only movie theater in town. Best I can figure, Howard sculpted about a quarter of a million heads and went through enough hair tonic to fill an oil tanker. Nellie stayed home and poured love into their four children and about five thousand red-velvet cakes.

Whenever Howard wasn't mowing hair—or the four acres of grass that grew on their riverfront lot—he was with Nellie. The only thing that ever separated them was his work. Other than that, they spent all their time together.

Three times a week, for over sixty years, they sat together in church, second row from the front, left side, holding hands. Seven nights a week they knelt together for prayers. Every day, they shared at least two meals.

Their marriage was for better or for worse. And it was mostly for better, until Nellie got older and began to lose her sight. But even that made them closer. Howard retired from barbering, bought her a phone with numbers the size of their great-grandchildren, took over the cooking, and sat even closer to Nellie in church—holding her by the arm instead of her hand. He was her light.

But then Howard died.

Nellie moved into a personal-care facility. Even with frequent visits from her children and grandchildren, her gray world became darker and sadder. It was hard to get her to eat. She became as weak as a newborn kitten.

One day, after months of waiting for Howard to walk back into the room, the rail-thin woman who hardly had the strength to open her eyes, bolted up in bed and declared in a strong voice, "Look at those people! They've got flowers all over them. They're smiling. Aren't they beautiful?"

Then she lay back down and died.

Some thought Howard had sent some of his new angel friends to go and get her, take her by the arm, and walk her back to his place. Others *knew* that's what happened. There would be no separating those two.

Not long after Nellie's death, I heard a song on the radio while driving to work that made me think about the love she and Howard had and now have again. Mind you, I don't listen to country music. But every so often some radio gnomes sneak into my car and change the settings. Anyway, the chorus described a couple much like Howard and Nellie. After a lifetime of being together, the wife finally died. Her husband found a note she had written years before. She wanted him to know that if she got to heaven before he did, she'd wait for him to finish his chores and join her. The final two lines were:

And between now and then, till I see you again,
I'll be loving you. Love, me.

Some may think Howard and Nellie were too close, enmeshed. Perhaps. But I don't think so. I think those two lovers were intertwined in a wonderful way. Like the members of the Trinity, they had become a community of constant companionship.

As the devotion masters tell us, our journey of transformation into Christ-likeness begins as we become willing to take the *time* to practice the presence of God and engage in soul-healing conversation. Developing a relationship with God is similar to developing a relationship like the one Nellie and Howard had with each other. No, it's exactly like that.

Howard and Nellie were a couple of ordinary mountain folks who "got it." They discovered a simple secret and acted on it—to realize the true value of the other and spend enormous amounts of time together.

Transforming love requires time and a vision of forever. At least until the flowery people come to walk us back to our garden home. That's the first requirement for falling head-over-heels in love with God. Now for the second.

COMMUNION BEGINS WITH HONESTY

Sharon's exclusive subdivision borders the desert. Her spacious home overlooks a picture-perfect golf course where her husband plays each day. Together they share a five-star world of fancy restaurants, afternoon tea at the club, and silk pillowcases. It's a long way from Howard and Nellie's world of Denny's, sweet tea in jelly glasses, and flannel pajamas.

Sharon's well-decorated home could appear on the pages of *Better Homes and Gardens*. The walls and tabletops witness that her husband is a successful businessman, and she is a popular writer and speaker. Most of her writing and speaking has been about God.

When I met her, Sharon's life was buffed and polished—at least on the outside. But on the inside, in the parts of her soul visible only to her and God, she often felt tarnished, unsuccessful, and afraid. Down deep was a chasm of anxiety and, at times, desperate loneliness. It was a pit in her soul so deep that she could fill it with trophies, books, a good husband, model children, and a picture-perfect life.

In spite of all Sharon had accomplished, in spite of always playing by the rules of external perfection, and in spite of all the words she had crafted about God's love, she often felt a dull ache that applause could not medicate. "This can't be all there is," she said as a mantra.

Then one day, while sitting in a seminar, she heard a song that she knew was written just for her, a song about the hole in the soul. A song about being homesick for a place you have never been before but want desperately to go.

Homesick for Eden*

A garden so green where water ran clean
And the animals roamed without names

Love was a girl who walked through the world
Where passion was pure as a flame

---

* Grateful acknowledgment is made for use of the lyrics to "Homesick for Eden," by Claire Cloninger/Paul Smith, © 1989 Word Music, LLC. All rights reserved. Used by permission.

In the back of our minds is a time before time
And a sad irreversible fact
We can't seem to think why we left there
And we can't seem to find our way back

All of us are homesick for Eden
We yearn to return to a land we've never known

Deep is the need to go back to the garden
A burning so strong for a place we belong
A place that we know is home

Have you ever just cried for no reason why
Like a child that's been left on it's own

You can't quite explain the confusion or pain
So you live with the heartache alone

In the back of your mind is a place and a time
And an image of what should have been

And you know that you'll never be happy
Until you find your way back there again

All of us are homesick for Eden
We yearn to return to a land we've never known

Deep is the need to go back to the garden
A burning so strong for a place we belong
A place that we know is home

We were made to live in his perfect love
We were meant to walk in his grace
And we'll never feel we are home again
Until we see him face to face

Deep is our need to go back to the garden,
A burning so strong for a place we belong
To rest at his feet in fellowship sweet
A place we know is home

When Sharon heard those words, she wanted to do something she had not tried before. She became ruthlessly honest with God. She told him that while she had admired him, she had never truly and recklessly loved him. She told him she had purposely kept him at arm's length for fear that he would either reject her or ask for more than she could give. And she even told him that she had harbored anger at him for not rescuing her from the abuse she suffered as a child.

And then, at the end of what turned into two days of crying, she asked him if he would reopen the gates of Eden, just for her, so she could step inside and live life the way he intended, in constant and loving relationship with him.

It took a lot of desperation for Sharon to say all that. But she did. And now, years later, she's still as sure as anything that God rewarded her honesty by saying yes as he pushed open the gate and took her by the hand.

Like Howard and Nellie, Sharon experienced a secret of transformation. Real change requires honesty about where we are right now and where we want to be. That's the second requirement for falling for God: to get real, to be totally honest about our predicament. There is nothing we can *achieve* that will fill the God-shaped void in the center of the soul. The smartest thing we can do is to lift our hands, like a small child wanting to be picked up by a parent, and say, "Help, me God. I'm lost and alone. Please pick me up. Hold me in your arms and tell me everything is going to be all right."

The third requirement for soul change can be the most difficult of all.

TRUSTING IN GOD'S DESIRE FOR INTIMACY

Fortunately, we are not the only ones who get homesick for the intimacy of Eden. God gets homesick too. Richard Foster begins his book *Prayer: Finding the Heart's True Home* with the following words:

> God has graciously allowed me to catch a glimpse into his heart, and
> I want to share with you what I have seen. Today the heart of God is
> an open wound of love. He aches over our distance and preoccupations.
> He mourns that we do not draw near to him. He grieves that we have
> forgotten him. He weeps over our obsession with much-ness and many-
> ness. He longs for our presence.
>
> And he is inviting you—and me—to come home, to come home to
> where we belong, to come home to that for which we were created. His
> arms are stretched out wide to receive us. His heart is enlarged to take
> us in.[1]

I've read and reread those words at least a hundred times. Even as I typed them, I felt a lump in my throat and a simultaneous sense of both disbelief and hope.

Could it be that the Creator of the entire universe aches with anticipation that I might return home to his presence? Could he really be facing in my direction with outstretched arms, calling my name, waving for me to come back home?

Yes, the most real part of me whispers and then suggests that the story of the prodigal son is the best image we have for the love of God. Let's consider these familiar words again, but this time, from the father's perspective.

You know the story by heart. The younger of two sons says to his father, in effect, "I wish you were dead so I could spend my inheritance."

The father doesn't punish the boy. Instead he divides his property between his two sons, sells half, and gives the money to the prodigal. The boy packs his bags and heads off to experience the world.

And experience it he does. He leaves no sensual craving unattended. It does not take him long to squander the entire inheritance. He is left penniless as a famine sweeps the country.

He signs on with a farmer who gives him the job of slopping pigs. By this point the prodigal is so hungry he would have eaten the corncobs in the pig slop, but no one will give him any.

In time the boy comes to his senses and recalls that even the farmhands working for his father sit down for three meals a day. So he swallows his pride and sets out to return home. He thinks, *I'll tell him I know I've sinned against him and God. I'll say, "I'm not fit to be called your son. But please take me on as a hired hand."*

Let's listen to how Luke describes what happens next.

When he was still a long way off, his father saw him. His heart pounding, he ran out, embraced him, and kissed him. The son started his speech: "Father, I've sinned against God, I've sinned before you; I don't deserve to be called your son ever again."

But the father wasn't listening. He was calling to the servants, "Quick. Bring a clean set of clothes and dress him. Put the family ring on his finger and sandals on his feet. Then get a grain-fed heifer and roast it. We're going to feast! We're going to have a wonderful time! My son is here—given up for dead and now alive! Given up for lost and now found!" And they began to have a wonderful time. (Luke 15:20-24, MSG, emphasis added)

There. Did you see it? The moment when the father isn't listening? Incredible! How can that be? Simple. He is completely distracted by his pounding heart—pounding at the possibility of a restored relationship with the one he so dearly loves. The joy of his child's presence makes the father deaf to further confession and blind to the pig slop on the boy's face.

And notice this. In the verse before this story, Jesus says that God, the Father in the story he is about to tell, is so much in love with his children—with you—that he throws a party with his angels every time one lost soul returns home.[2]

Yes, if you've already left your personal pigpen of self-sufficiency, you have been the cause of a heavenly bash. Heaven partied the day you said, "Enough, I was wrong to try to be God. I've made a mess of my life. I want to apologize and go home."

And then, before you had time to arrive, there he was, your heavenly Father, scanning the horizon, looking for a sign that you were coming back. And when he saw you—a speck in the distance—he broke into a run, so undignified for a patriarch, and hugged you as you tried futilely to explain. He was too distracted by his excitement to listen. Did you feel it? Do you want to feel it now?

Because I know this story is timeless, I can confess to God and to you that my soul is darkly stained by the choice of Adam and Eve. I've made the same wrong choice, and continue to make it, hundreds of times each day. Even though I've read the script written by the prodigal son, I continue to play his role myself. And as if this weren't bad enough, I've accepted the forgiveness of my heavenly Father, felt his embrace, only to get up the next morning, pack my bags, and leave again and again and again. Maybe seventy times seven. Maybe more. Over and over I choose control, perfectionism, drive for success, and myself over trust, acceptance, enjoyment of the present moment, and God.

Yet I sense that I am loved—in this very moment—beyond what my mind can possibly contain. Not only is my homesickness for loving community a homing device that calls to my soul, but also, I truly believe, God is homesick for me, and desires to spend endless amounts of his time with me, talking with me, and just being with me for the joy of relationship. In this I place my hope—in his desire for intimacy with me.

I want to confess again, "I've eaten from the wrong tree. I've returned to the slop of self-rule." I'm saying it out loud. But my Father isn't listening to me. His heart is pounding too loudly with anticipation of my return.

What kind of love is this? A love stronger than my fear and arrogance. Eventually I will become so transformed by his desire for relationship that I will want to stay home forever. I will feel the change of inner transformation. Even now the slop of independence and self-rule looks more like slop, and a relationship to God, like the pearl of great price.

God, my Daddy, is Fall-proofing my soul for all eternity by his desire for intimacy, his delirious love, and his offer of relationship. He wants to hug me so tightly that we become one and I never again choose to run. He wants the same for you.

Transformation is a process of falling in love with God. It requires three things: time for *conversation,* honesty that leads to *communion,* and trust that God's desire for *consummation* will not be thwarted. Our deepest desires are amplified in the pounding heart of God and will lead us from the presence of pigs to union with him.

LET'S BE PRACTICAL: THE CRUMBS AND BUBBLES OF CHANGE

For most of us the incremental journey back to falling in love with God can resemble the winding loops of a toy Slinky more than a straight line. Because of this, it's important to develop an appreciation for small changes.

A story by Safed the Sage helps me understand this. William E. Barton was one of America's preeminent clergymen. He wrote more than sixty books, and his influence was able to leapfrog denominational boundaries. During the last fifteen years of his life he wrote a series of parables using the pen name Safed the Sage. The genius of these stories rested in Safed's ability to find timeless truth in daily incidents.

My favorite of Barton's parables is called "Crumbs and Bubbles." It's the best illustration I've ever found for appreciating the slow but sure process of real change.

As the parable begins, Safed is spending a quiet day with his granddaughter when it begins to snow. The little girl looks out the window and notices the fluffy, falling flakes. She asks her grandfather to take her outside to play in the snow, and he cannot refuse.

Once outside, the little girl begins to giggle with delight as the snow comes down. She says, "Look, Grandpa, the snow is making crumbs and bubbles."

When he asks her what she means by crumbs and bubbles, she explains, "The bubbles are falling against your face, Grandpa, and turn to water. But the crumbs land on your overcoat. They don't melt and you can brush them off. Watch."

Safed marvels at the way the small child put the words together to describe her new experiences. They spend the day enjoying the crumbs and bubbles until the cold sends them inside to thaw by a crackling fire.

The next morning he awakens and notices how quiet everything has become. There is no movement outside, no noise from trains, cars, or footsteps. He looks out the window and observes that the snow has fallen in great drifts and brought the entire town to a halt.

Then he remembers the cute words of his granddaughter and how she describes the crumbs and bubbles of snow, which now have piled up in such great drifts that they can stop a powerful train.

Then Safed unpacks the parable. He says, "I considered that it is even so with many things in life that are small in themselves, but when multiplied they become habits that people cannot break, or grievances that rend friendships asunder, even as great drifts are made of bubbles and crumbs of snow."[3]

And, I would add, so it is with the crumbs and bubbles of Christian formation. These are the disciplines, the little things we can do that make us more aware of God's loving presence. In and of themselves, these things can seem so small and insignificant. A few minutes here to meditate on a passage of Scripture, a few there to stop and just be with God, listening for his voice, a moment before surrendering to sleep to inventory the day and examine our conscience, being honest about a lack of desire, asking for help in trusting his love. So small, yes, but they can pile up in drifts great enough to stop a runaway ego.

Crumbs and bubbles are the things we can do each day by direct effort that make it possible to do what we could never accomplish by direct effort: the transformation of our will, thought, emotion, behavior, and social interaction through inward surrender to God's internal presence.

Falling in love with God and allowing our relationship with him to deepen through taking the time for the tiny disciplines of affection can lead us down the path to ultimate union. Real change happens through the development of a romantic relationship with God. And it happens one crumb and one bubble at a time.

~~~~~

Bible Study: The Wedding Feast at Cana

Text: John 2:1-10

> On the third day a wedding took place at Cana in Galilee. Jesus' mother was there, and Jesus and his disciples had also been invited to the wedding. When the wine was gone, Jesus' mother said to him, "They have no more wine."

19

"Dear woman, why do you involve me?" Jesus replied. "My time has not yet come."

His mother said to the servants, "Do whatever he tells you."

Nearby stood six stone water jars, the kind used by the Jews for ceremonial washing, each holding from twenty to thirty gallons.

Jesus said to the servants, "Fill the jars with water"; so they filled them to the brim.

Then he told them, "Now draw some out and take it to the master of the banquet."

They did so, and the master of the banquet tasted the water that had been turned into wine. He did not realize where it had come from, though the servants who had drawn the water knew. Then he called the bridegroom aside and said, "Everyone brings out the choice wine first and then the cheaper wine after the guests have had too much to drink; but you have saved the best till now."

Observations

Jesus had a lot of time to think about this moment. He waited for a very long time after the Fall before stepping into human history, and then he waited thirty more years before beginning his public ministry. Eons plus thirty years to consider this moment, the event of his first miracle. I don't think it's an accident that he chooses a wedding feast for the backdrop—after all, the church would come to be referred to as his bride, and he, the Groom. But something else seems to be going on here, something symbolic, mystical. It's no surprise that John, the mystic, is the only gospel writer to cover this breaking story. Jesus asks for six earthen vessels containing twenty to thirty gallons of water each. A gallon of water weighs in at about eight pounds. The filled earthen vessels at Cana weighed between 160 and 240 pounds. That describes a lot of people I know.

With wedding images in the background, Jesus takes center stage and kicks off his public ministry by radically changing the contents of earthen vessels. Spirit is added, and plain water becomes extraordinary wine. Transformation. Jesus' first miracle foreshadows all that will follow. It's about radical changes to the contents of earthen vessels. Water to wine. Saul to Paul. You to Jesus.

Reflection Questions

1. How do you respond to the idea that Jesus intentionally chose a wedding for the setting of his first miracle?
2. In what way might the miracle of Cana also foreshadow the sacrament of Holy Communion? *Hint:* How does communion symbolize the mystery of "Christ in me" and changing the contents of earthen vessels?
3. Does the content of your earthen vessel seem more like water or wine right now? Why? What can you do to help bring about a change— or to continue to be brimming with the good stuff?

Meditation: A Historic Model for Change

Explanation

I believe that all the great revival movements of church history began and spread as a result of an experience of real change within the souls of believers. From Calvin to Wesley and from Keswick to Azusa Street, we find magnificent accounts of transformed lives, souls aflame with the presence and love of God.

But then it happens, it always happens, the statistical concept known as regression to the mean. The gravitational pull of the world against all who would soar above.

With the passing years, flames of love often begin to flicker and turn into smoldering ashes. The joy of salvation may be reduced to the sterile, contractual security of having a fire insurance policy with God. The drag of complacency often slows sanctification into merely making efforts to avoid the behaviors in column B—instead of being empty of self and bubbling with the new wine of Christ's love. For many, Spirit baptism comes to mean speaking in tongues instead of daily producing the lush fruit of the Spirit, the very character of Christ.

unshackle

In all of church history only a small number of saints and apostles have been able to find a way to blast beyond the powerful pull of regression to the world's mean. Their secret, I believe, is no secret at all. Saints are just like you and I—except they have determined to live their lives so close to God that it makes the devil too nervous to follow. Since they are walking that close to the Author of Life, they talk with him. Saints dialogue with God—keeping a conversation going throughout the day—until the relationship deepens into communion and communion leads to union.

One last thing before presenting our initial meditation exercise. Instead of using words like *saved* or *sanctified* (good words—but words that can become too familiar and thus diminished), the early church described the process of spiritual transformation as a lifelong pilgrimage of *purgation* (releasing those things that pull us away from God), *illumination* (receiving what draws us close to him), and *union* (Christ fully integrated into the fabric of our soul until our wills, minds, emotions, behaviors, and social interactions are one.) This beautiful language resists static complacency.

In this section of each chapter I will offer a brief presentation of a meditation designed to amplify the section and chapter theme of conversation, communion, or union while focusing on one of the three classic movements of transformation: purgation (releasing), illumination (receiving), or union (integration). This is done to imitate the wisdom of the early church and as a way to weave practical suggestions into each chapter.

Meditation

Richard J. Foster has made popular a simple meditation that highlights the meaning and experience of purgation and illumination. It goes like this:

Sit in a comfortable position and allow your mind to become quiet and your breathing to deepen. After a few minutes of becoming centered, place your hands in your lap with your palms facing down—signifying a willingness to let go or release things that impede your journey of transformation. As you continue to breath slowly and deeply, say to the rhythm of your breathing, "Lord, I release my attachments to everything in life that distracts me from spending time with you." Perhaps a few specific things will come to mind, and you will name them before God as you continue to hold your palms face down.

Then after a time of releasing, perhaps three to ten minutes, turn your palms face up and pray as you breathe, "Lord, I receive from you a deeper awareness of your presence in my life." Stay with this for three to ten minutes, but attempt to carry the attitude of awareness throughout the day.

Spiritual Exercise: The Five Ps of Prayer

Explanation

This exercise appears first because of its foundational nature. Other exercises in this book will be based on your having a foundational understanding of these Five Ps of Prayer. Slowly read through the Five Ps of Prayer and then incorporate each into the prayer exercise that follows.

Place

Find a *place* for prayer that is quiet, comfortable, and free from distractions. Any old monastery will do—as will your living room, den, or office at certain times of the day. There must be no chance, however, of being disturbed.

Position

Place yourself in a comfortable physical *position.* It will be better if neither your arms nor legs are crossed. Sitting in a straight-back posture is best. Stretched out on the floor or bed will only work for true insomniacs. Recliners are death to prayer.

Pace

Slow the *pace* of your breathing to four to seven deep breaths per minute.

Take deep, slow, and diaphragmatic breaths. Do this by keeping your chest relatively still as your lungs fill with air and your belly expands. It may help to place your hand over your stomach and feel it push out as you inhale.

After learning how it feels to breathe deeply by expanding your diaphragm, count as you slowly breathe in and out. That is, slowly count from one to four as you breathe in. Hold the breath for a count of one, two, or three (whatever feels most comfortable). Then breathe out as you slowly count from one to four and pause for a moment before you repeat the process.

Perceptions

As you set the stage for listening or contemplative prayer, don't seek for anything sensational. Instead, limit yourself to observing. Become aware of sensations—the touch of your clothes on your shoulders, your clothes on your back, or your back touching the chair you are sitting on. Be aware of sensations coming to you from your hands, feet, and legs. Feel the temperature of the room and any warm or cool movements of air. Focus your perceptions on your body and senses. For contemplative or listening prayer, it is essential to make contact with the present and stay there.

Resist the temptation to seek novelty of experience. Instead, seek depth of awareness. When thoughts come to your mind, resist the temptation to follow them around. Also resist the temptation to become frustrated by your thoughts. Instead, observe them as someone stationed by an open window might watch passersby on the street. Or as you might passively observe ascending balloons. But keep a stationary, observing posture.

Return often to the sensation of your slow, deep breathing. Focus on the tips of your nostrils and feel the coolness as you breathe in, the warmth as you breathe out.

Purpose

Remember that the aim of prayer is to enter into conversation with God. It is not restricted to certain hours of the day. A Christian can feel herself in the presence of God. The goal of prayer is precisely to be with God always.

Exercise

Find a time and place to begin experiencing the Five Ps of Prayer for at least fifteen to twenty minutes. After taking some time to quiet yourself and rest in the presence of God, initiate a conversation with him about the theme of this chapter: "First I've got to admit it's broken."

Part 1

Conversation

Talking to God
Without Losing Your Mind

Chapter 2

Becoming Open to Love

Understanding the Kingdom of God

> *If I find in myself a desire which no experience in this world can satisfy, the most probable explanation is that I was made for another world.*
>
> C. S. LEWIS

The imagery of the Garden of Eden portrays God's intent for humanity. Adam and Eve were a prince and a princess, living in the King's backyard. Their relationship with God and each other was to be happily ever after—intimate, conversational, and communal. All they had to do to keep paradise found was to live in obedience—human will in union with divine intention. But they screwed up and discovered that autonomy comes with a staggering price. Adam and Eve did two things that severed their relationship with God. Seeds of distrust planted in their souls ripened and caused each first to *grasp* and then to *hide*.[1]

In *grasping* from the wrong tree, they voted that they cherished control, independence, and self-determination more than surrender, community, and abandonment to the love of God. In *hiding* they moved into a world of shame and isolation and out of the realm of grace and togetherness.

These two themes—grasping and hiding—have soiled the souls of every descendent of Adam and Eve. They block us from being in position for conversation, communion, and union with God. Grasping and hiding yank us away from Eden and into a world of competition, loneliness, and silent desperation, an unnatural world for the human soul. Instead of living in God's garden of delight, most of the sons of Adam and daughters of Eve live in cramped little fiefdoms of their own creation.

Our journey back to God's arms is always the path from life in our kingdom of "grasp" and "hide" to life in God's kingdom of "surrender" and "embrace." But before most of us would be willing even to attempt such a journey, we need at least three ideas planted in our hearts:

1. The invisible, right-side-up kingdom that Jesus described actually exists all around us as the new Eden.
2. The central mission of Jesus during his time on earth was to teach about the present availability of this kingdom and to demonstrate his right to do so.
3. We can enter into the kingdom here and now if we are willing to approach it as a small child.

But for any of this to make much sense, we need a new perspective on the kingdom of God and why it was of utmost significance in the life and teaching of Jesus. I know how powerful this gaining a new perspective can be. It happened for me several years ago.

THE NEW EDEN

From the Garden of Eden into Plato's Cave

It was a springtime Saturday morning, and I was sitting in a converted Sunday-school classroom in the underbelly of a large church in southern California. Cardboard cutouts of smiling disciples and a laughing Jesus brightly decorated the four walls. I assumed the room would be filled with a pack of energetic five-year-olds the next morning. But it was Saturday, and the crowd I was with was not that young and bubbly—forty frowning, dully decorated seminarians. I was at this remote seminary outpost because I needed one last theology class to graduate.

The professor entered the room. He was smiling so broadly that he seemed to belong up on the wall with Jesus and the disciples instead of down on the tile floor with the rest of us. He started unpacking his briefcase, surrounding himself with orderly piles of books and folders. He didn't need to go to all that trouble for me. I could already tell him what I wanted from the course. I wanted the words of his lecture notes to be transferred to my blank, yellow legal pad and then back onto his final exam paper in the most painless way possible.

His methodological search led him to a videotape. He seemed very pleased with the find and placed it in the machine and turned the lights off and the volume up. Within seconds, crudely drawn animated figures were peering at us from the television screen. Life was as it should be. It was Saturday morning, and I was watching cartoons.

But it wasn't Pluto. It was Plato. To be more precise, it was Plato's cave. Still, I wasn't complaining. The content mesmerized.

The camera focused first on the faces of four prisoners. They were laughing and pointing straight ahead. Then the camera panned back and revealed that chains bound each prisoner in such a manner that it would be impossible for him to stand or to look behind.

These prisoners lived in a large underground cave, and the only thing they were allowed to see was the back of their Flintstonian home. Behind them, at the mouth of the cave, a huge fire burned. It threw light against the wall they faced.

On a raised platform between the fire and the prisoners, people marched back and forth carrying wooden carvings of objects—trees, flowers, birds, and the like—high over their heads. These people were too far away for the prisoners to hear their voices or footsteps clearly. The objects paraded in front of the fire cast shadows on the back wall, making the prisoners a captive theater audience without popcorn.

The shadows on the wall of the cave were the only reality the prisoners knew. The cave dwellers had made a contest of naming the shadows and pre-dicting the patterns of their appearance. The prisoners became quite good at these interpretations and predictions. Indeed, they adopted the custom of offering an award to the one who was best at the game.

Then one day (of course the cellmates knew nothing of the concept of "day") someone entered the cave and descended to where the prisoners were kept in a single-file, shoulder-to-shoulder row. He approached them, knelt behind one, touched his chains, and they fell to the floor. The now-freed pris-oner awkwardly stood to his feet. The one who had done the freeing attempted to explain about the cave and the outside world. But it was difficult to com-municate with someone who could speak only Shadowese.

Reluctantly, the former prisoner allowed himself to be led up the steep ascent to the mouth of the cave, where upon arrival, he grabbed at his eyes in pain because of the brightness of the sun. He had never seen it before, and its burning reality caused his eyes to squint and then his eyelids to slam shut. He had to be held to keep from running back to the safety of the dark cave. He did not realize he was a butterfly finally set free from a cocoon, a life born again.

In time he slowly adapted to the light. It wasn't long before he was able to see real trees, flowers, and birds. In even less time, the truth began to dawn on him. His world had been a prison, which contained only the shadows of real-ity, the reality of life in full.

The former prisoner began to run and play like an excited child. He put his feet in real water, inhaled the fragrance of real flowers, and heard the melody of a choir of real birds. For the first time ever, he was filled with joy. That is, until he remembered the other prisoners.

His compassion for his friends pushed him back to the mouth of the cave. There he decided that he must descend into the cave and help free the others, even though he hated to miss one moment in the real world.

When he arrived back in their presence, all of them could see that he had changed. He had grown accustomed to the outside world, to light, and to freedom. The shadows on the wall appeared fuzzy to him now, and he had forgotten the games of trivial pursuit—predicting the shadow patterns.

The others saw his difficulty and concluded that he was in need of a straitjacket. Instead of welcoming his offer of freedom, they laughed at the messenger and decided he should be put to death. Fortunately for him, they were chained. With slow steps the would-be-messiah left the jeers and taunts and ascended again to the real world, thinking to himself, *Better to be the poor servant of a poor master outside the cave than to think and live as them.*

The projector sputtered to a stop, and the professor turned the lights back on in our cave. He asked only, "So, what do you think?"

While others became animated and responded for almost an hour, I sat in stunned silence as a documentary was filmed on location, in my head.

What did I think? I thought that I had just sat in a twentieth-century church and witnessed the telling of a pre-Christian parable by a troupe of cartoon characters, causing a floodlight to turn on in my mind. The life and the mission of Christ had finally become illuminated.

How had I missed all the cave and kingdom language in Scripture? Didn't Jesus begin his earthly ministry with the announcement that he had entered into our cave, the world, to set the captives free, to restore sight to the blind, to proclaim the good news that there is another world all around us, and it is called the kingdom of God? The contrast between the world and the kingdom had never been drawn so clearly for me.

Other parallels began to pop into my mind:

- Jesus was put to death by those whose secure reality was challenged by his talk of the "outside world" of his kingdom.
- The good news of the gospel of Jesus is here-and-now good news.

So often we live our lives more in line with the grasping principles of the cave rather than the letting-go principles of the kingdom. We play earthly shadow games of politics, power, and possessions rather than risk the vulnerability of selfless love, willingness, and simplicity.

Yes, I thought, *we have indeed fallen from the Garden of Eden and into Plato's cave. We live in an unnatural environment, one for which we were not designed. And for all the talk of abundant life and the kingdom of God, our reality is most often that of rock and shadow, grasp and hide.*

I would like to go outside now, I continued to think. *Not outside the classroom, but outside the cave.* I looked up at the cardboard cutout of Jesus and the disciples. *So that's why they're all smiling! There really is something to be joyful about.* As I thought that, I'm pretty sure I saw Jesus wink. I think he loves it when we catch a glimpse of his vision of the world.

Getting a Vision of Forever

Fast forward from about 370 B.C., a likely date for Plato's *Republic,* which contains the parable of the cave, through twenty-four centuries of stories, parables, and fairy tales about the desire of fallen princes and princesses to be reinstated in glowing kingdoms, to the spring of 1999 when the film *The Matrix* was released.

The Wachowski brothers, Andy and Larry, wrote and directed *The Matrix.* These names don't have the same ring as Plato, but their vision for the unseen real is just as keen.

The film opens in the year 2199. The human race has become enslaved to man-made machines armed with artificial intelligence. To keep humans under control, the machines place them in the Matrix, a highly advanced computer simulation program that creates what is experienced as the real world.

Human beings live their daily lives in this computer-generated dream world without any knowledge that theirs is a false existence. Most of the characters are as convinced as the prisoners in Plato's cave that what they see, hear, feel, taste, and smell is the real world. But it is not. The real world is outside their realm of understanding.

As the plot develops, some rebel humans discover the horror of their ephemeral existence and recruit the help of a computer hacker, appropriately named Neo ("new man"). They hope that he will be "the one" to rescue the world from this cyber-slavery, from the oppression of a false reality.

Morpheus ("I will be what I will be") is the father image, the champion of Zion, a city where humans live in reality—outside the Matrix. Morpheus is the leader of the rebel forces and is determined that his people will be set free through the chosen one, Neo.

The third prominent character is Trinity (I'm not making this up). She helps Neo, provides him counsel, and is capable of supernatural fight and flight. If Morpheus can be the father/God image, and Neo the dual-nature/Son image, then Trinity is the Spirit. Together the three will work to set the captives free and restore sight to the blind.

And these are just the beginning of the biblical references—there is also a spaceship named Nebuchadnessar and a resurrection. But these are not the parallels that prompt this reference to *The Matrix*.

Like Plato's parable of the cave, the Wachowskis' parable is about two worlds, one visible and the other not, and prisoners—who see through the glass dimly, if at all—who populate the visible world. In both stories what appears real is not, and all that really matters is what exists just beyond the reach of one's senses. Only when the captives become willing to have their chains unlocked (or our brains unplugged) do they begin to see clearly and become motivated to follow the path that leads to an experience of the genuine.

This is exactly how it is for you and me. Our true home, the kingdom of God, is generally beyond the boundaries of our awareness.

Plato's cave and *The Matrix* reveal the truth about our present existence as well as the first step necessary for the restoration of an intimate relationship with God. *We need to doubt our present and visible reality (a "cave" or "matrix" type of existence) as the ultimate reality and then catch a vision of the really real. The real that lasts forever.*

Authentic transformation requires a vision of the invisible, right-side-up kingdom that Jesus described and the belief that we can live there, both here and now *and* there and later. And because Jesus devoted much of his attention to life in the kingdom, we must learn how to live there as well.

THE CENTRAL TEACHING OF JESUS

For Jesus, a carpenter's son from an obscure village, to offer an invitation to come out of the darkness and live right-side-up lives makes no sense to many, then or now. Indeed, his mission only comes into focus against a backdrop of the reality of two radically different worlds—cave versus kingdom, matrix versus reality.

Jesus entered our world like an outsider into Plato's cave, like Neo bursting out of the Matrix. He came to show and teach about the life for which we were designed but had not experienced since the Garden of Eden. He came to open access to a new realm of existence—life in community with God, under the governance of the king. By relying on our reestablished relationship with him, we are now able to reintegrate the little realm that makes up our life into his infinite kingdom. Jesus is the door, means, and methodology for living life by original intent—free from fear, free from grasping and hiding.

However unlikely it seems to us, God designed us for the task of ruling and reigning with him by framing our nature to function best only in a conscious, personal, and interactive relationship with him. Somewhere deep within, we know that and recognize the kingdom as our true culture.

But we are meant to exercise our "rule" only as we walk in union with God. To do so is to find the kingdom and our place within. To do so is nothing less than a new birth into a radically different world of infinite possibilities.

Some conclude that Jesus was so singularly focused that he only did three things during his time on earth. One, he introduced the kingdom of God as a here-and-now reality, inviting all who would listen to the grand reopening. Two, he described the ethics and principles of the kingdom and placed them in marked contrast to the ways of the world. (See, for example, the Sermon on the Mount, Matthew 5–7, and his commencement address to the disciples,

John 13–17.) Three, he demonstrated through signs and wonders his right to teach so authoritatively. His death and resurrection were the ultimate proof that his promises could be cashed like checks from Bill Gates.

"This is the time of fulfillment. The kingdom of God is at hand," Jesus boldly announced to a quiet gathering in a synagogue in his hometown. "Repent and believe the gospel." (See Luke 4:16-30.)

But what is the gospel? What is the news that is so good it is worth having the Son of God empty himself of celestial glory to face diaper rash, splinters, betrayal by friends, and death on a cross? According to Dallas Willard, Jesus' desire to announce the reality and availability of life in the kingdom made his suffering worth it. The availability of life in the kingdom is this "good news."

Jesus' presence on earth was the reality and availability of the kingdom, here and now, later and forever. Living in the kingdom is the most important thing a person can do and should be the supreme object of human striving.[2]

John Bright, the gifted Old Testament scholar, wrote a classic called *The Kingdom of God.* He, like Willard, perceived that the central theme in Scripture is salvation to life in the kingdom. Not just salvation *from* hell, but salvation *to* a whole new reality—both in the present and forever. Bright says that the concept of the kingdom is the total message of the gospel: To understand the kingdom is to understand salvation, and to misunderstand the significance of the kingdom is to misunderstand salvation.

Then what are we saved from? We are saved from the darkness of the cave, a life of self-rule, grasping, hiding, and isolation, to a life of living in interactive relationship with God. Salvation means a recovery of the lost Eden, the kingdom of God, and the possibility of a transforming friendship with God.

But What Is the Kingdom?
Okay, okay, but what is it? What is the kingdom?

The kingdom of God means the kingly rule or dominion of God, the sole ruler of the universe. His rules rule his subjects. In the kingdom the will of the subjects unites with the will of the king. It is restoration of active and intimate relationship with God. It is life outside the boundaries of what appears real.

Taking our place in the kingdom means coming home to Eden. Coming home to conversation, communion, and union with God and one another.

In God's kingdom, love, humility, and a sense of *we*-ness dominate the lives of his subjects rather than the fear, pride, and me-ness that characterizes life in the cave. We stay in the kingdom by staying "in Christ," just as he recommended to his disciples in the priestly prayer of John 17. To be in the kingdom is to be in Christ, organically connected to him like branches into the vine that birthed them and one with both him and the Father.

But how do I know if I'm there?

The Imagery of Birth

To answer the question of whether we are living life in the kingdom, consider the new-birth imagery Jesus introduced in John 3. Before being born, a child lives in a tiny cave—her mother's womb—that is dark, warm, and safe. The outside world is known only through muffled noise.

Then the baby's world is turned upside down. Pain, discomfort, loud noises, an explosion of light, and a cruel slap of reality shatter the comfortable life of the cave. The outside world is a fearful place, a nightmare. But then it happens: the sight of mother's smiling face, the touch of skin, loving words, food with taste, and a glowing world the size of infinity waiting to be discovered.

To know if you are living life in the kingdom, ask yourself this question: Is my new life in Christ as different from my former life as life outside the womb is from life inside? To the extent that this contrast is minimal, so has been our full experience of life outside the cave.

For those, like me, who came to Christ at a young age and have no "before" and "after" pictures, the better question is, Do I value the things Christ values—love, humility, and community—to a dramatically different level than those who remain chained to the world?

I began this chapter by saying that the journey back to the arms of God follows the path from life in our kingdom of grasp and hide to God's kingdom of surrender and embrace. Such a journey will require us to believe that the realm Jesus described actually exists and that his central mission was to encourage all of God's prodigal children to return home, to live in the kingdom.

This can all sound pretty intimidating. Even if I crave life in the kingdom, how do I get there? Where are the entrance ramps? Fortunately, Jesus reminds us that our return to Eden can be child's play. We can live here and now in the kingdom of God by becoming willing to be as a child—lost in excitement over all the possibilities for joy. Let me tell you a story about a little boy who showed me how easy it can be.

DANCIN' BOY

When time and money permit, my family likes to plan vacations by allowing each person to pick the place he or she most wants to visit and then connecting the dots. Prince Edward Island made the itinerary because one of my two daughters watched *Anne of Green Gables* until the pictures fell off the videotape. Naturally, she would want to see the place that inspired the author.

We were staying at a bed-and-breakfast that was part of a working farm—with pigs to be slopped, cows to be milked, and sheep hooked directly to a loom. The farm was a few hundred feet behind one of the only three colleges of piping in the world. I assumed it was a school that taught plumbers how to connect pipe and wear their pants, but I was wrong.

Our first morning there, I awoke to the sound of a cat being strangled. The noise went on for what seemed like hours. I was just about to get up and go help the cat fight back when my wife said, "Don't you just love bagpipes?"

About as much as I love a rousing polka or an ice-cream headache, I thought. Then it dawned on me. We were staying within earshot of a place where they train wannabe bagpipers. No wonder they only allow three of these colleges in the world. Probably tightly controlled by the United Nations.

That evening, however, we found ourselves sitting in an audience of a Celtic arts festival. Fortunately, the teachers at the college put it on, and it was outstanding. Two hours of Celtic folk songs, river dances, drums, and fiddling made the occasional cat strangling tolerable.

At one point, while a three-piece band was at full throttle, the drummer broke rank and stepped to center stage. He put on the most amazing display of percussion I had ever witnessed. His hands became invisible for four or five minutes.

Then it happened. A little boy, who looked to be about two or three, got up from his seat on the second row and walked over to the stage. He stared up at the drummer with open-mouthed amazement, his Irish-red hair touching the back of a kelly green T-shirt. As the music ascended, his little body could no longer hold it inside and began to percolate with excitement, then erupted in a highly original dance. His style compensated for his lack of rhythm.

The little boy was oblivious to the crowd. He threw his head even further back and began to twirl in circles. He clapped his hands, stamped his feet, and became a scarecrow in the funnel of a tornado.

The drummer noticed the dancing boy and locked his eyes on him. The boy noticed being noticed, and an instant bond formed. It was as if the two were the only ones present.

The drummer began to play even faster—just for the boy. And the boy danced faster—just for the joy. In one spontaneous moment, a thousand years of cultural history that previously lay dormant in a three-foot-tall body suddenly awakened and rushed out.

In that same moment, I realized what Jesus must have meant when he said all who truly discover the kingdom must do so as a small child. Yes, exactly as this dancing boy. To enter the kingdom is to recognize the cadence of our true culture and step away from where we have been seated. With the glorious freedom of a child, we abandon ourselves to its rhythms and become free from the opinions of others. To enter the kingdom is to become lost in the gaze of the One who is making the music, knowing that it is being played just for you.

Life back inside God's kingdom is so available a child can lead us. We delight in the joy of our true culture. And in the dancing swirl of a few moments of life in the kingdom, letting go replaces grasping, and intimacy trumps isolation.

Falling in love with God in a manner that can produce radical transformation requires the belief that all fairy tales are true. There is a realm of happily ever after. It exists now, all around us. Clicking our heels won't get us there, but the faith of a child will. See for yourself. Close your eyes. Listen for the music. Ask God to show you around.

Bible Study: The Kingdom of God

*Text: Matthew 4:13-17; 6:31-33; John 3:3;
Romans 14:17*

He went and lived in Capernaum, which was by the lake in the area of Zebulun and Naphtali—to fulfill what was said through the prophet Isaiah:

"Land of Zebulun and land of Naphtali,
the way to the sea, along the Jordan,

Galilee of the Gentiles—
the people living in darkness
    have seen a great light;
on those living in the land of the shadow of death
    a light has dawned."

From that time on Jesus began to preach, "Repent for the kingdom of heaven is near."

So do not worry, saying, "What shall we eat?" or "What shall we drink?" or "What shall we wear?" For the pagans run after all these things, and your heavenly Father knows that you need them. But seek first his kingdom and his righteousness, and all these things will be given to you as well.

In reply Jesus declared, "I tell you the truth, no one can see the kingdom of God unless he is born again."

For the kingdom of God is not a matter of eating and drinking, but of righteousness, peace and joy in the Holy Spirit.

Observations

Jesus came into our artificial world to release captives, restore true vision, and proclaim the great day of exodus. He came to reopen Eden's gate.

The kingdom of heaven is here and now, all around. God uniquely designed you to live there. You are meant to walk in union with God and learn from him how to rule with him. To journey from the world to the kingdom is nothing less than a new birth into a radically different realm of infinite possibilities.

Reflection Questions

✓1. How do you respond to the idea that the kingdom of God is near?

2. What are some practical steps you can take toward seeking the kingdom of God—above all else—on a daily, weekly, and monthly basis?

3. Describe your entry into God's kingdom.

4. What does it mean to you personally to say that you are living now in the realm of righteousness, peace, and joy?

Meditation: A Fish Named Homer

Explanation

A story has tumbled out of the Appalachian Mountains about a boy who decided to make a pet out of a fish he caught.[3] When he noticed that it was still alive after hours in the mountain air, he got the idea that he might be able to train it to breathe like dogs and cats.

The boy named his new pet Homer and worked with him each day—keeping it out of water for longer and longer periods of time. Eventually Homer learned to stay out of the water full time. The boy and Homer became fast friends. They were inseparable. This worked just fine until school started back up in the fall.

The fish tried to follow the boy to school—walking on his fins through the grass and dirt. The boy tried to get Homer to go back home, but he wouldn't listen. Even when the boy stomped his foot and threw a rock, Homer was determined.

Just before he got to the schoolhouse, the boy crossed a wooden bridge that had a few planks rotted out and missing. He kept walking but soon noticed that there were not any swishing noises behind him. He turned around and did not see Homer anywhere. He walked back over the bridge. No Homer. And then he looked down through a place on the bridge where a plank was missing. There was Homer. In the creek. Drowned.

~~~~~~

I am like Homer. I'm a fish out of water. More at home now in a false environment than the one for which I was created, and if I were suddenly tossed back into my original habitat, I might drown.

The purpose of this exercise and the one that follows is to provide slow and systematic training for learning how to adapt to the kingdom.

Meditation

Sit in a comfortable position and allow your mind to become quiet and your breathing, slow and deep.

After a few minutes of becoming more focused and at rest, place your hands in your lap with your palms facing down, as was described in the meditation section of chapter 1. This is done to signify a willingness to let go or release things that impede your journey of transformation.

As you continue to breathe slowly and deeply, pray to the rhythm of your breathing, *Lord, I release my attachments to all things that are not of your kingdom. Please bring to mind the things fear causes me to grasp for security or significance.*

Then, as each attachment comes to mind, pray silently and to the rhythm of your breathing, *Lord, I let go of* ———, *and I confess that it is a mere shadow of what you provide for me.*

Then after a time (perhaps three to ten minutes) of releasing things that you may be tempted to grasp as God-substitutes, turn your attention to the notion of hiding, and pray, *Lord, I confess to you that my shame has often caused me to hide from your presence. I also confess to you that feeling guilty has caused me to move away from you instead of toward you. With my palms down, I release this shame to you and ask that you would give me the courage to come out of hiding.*

Conclude the meditation by turning your palms up and praying as you breathe slowly and deeply, *Lord, I receive from you a deeper awareness of your presence in my life and a clearer vision for living in your kingdom. Make me like a fish back in the ocean of your kingdom. Teach me once again how to swim.*

Spiritual Exercise: Slowing Down to Experience God

A Reminder

Begin by taking five to ten minutes to monitor and experience the Five Ps of Prayer. You may want to turn back to pages 23–25 to review the more detailed list, or you may wish to simply glance at the reminder of the Five Ps presented below.

- *Place.* Find a quiet place that will remain free from distractions for twenty to thirty minutes.
- *Position.* Place yourself in a comfortable physical position.
- *Pace.* Gradually slow the rhythm of your breathing four to seven breaths per minute.
- *Perceptions.* Use your five senses as a checklist to make sure you are available to and aware of your perceptions. As you sit quietly with eyes closed, what do you feel, hear, see (mentally), taste, and smell?
- *Purpose.* Remember that the purpose for quiet, listening prayer is to enter into conversation with God.

Exercise

The following exercise can help you to become more deeply aware of the reality of God's omnipresence and to foster communication with him. You may wish to read it through several times before going through it mentally. Or you may wish to read it one sentence at a time and allow time to experience what is suggested.

- Close your eyes and practice the awareness of body sensations for a while.
- Then, become aware of your breathing by focusing first on the movements of your diaphragm and then through the alternating sensations of coolness and warmth (at the tips of your nostrils) as you breathe in and out.
- Reflect now that the air you are breathing in is charged with the power and presence of God. Think of the air that surrounds you as an immense ocean that is heavily colored with God's being. Consider that as you are drawing air into your lungs, you are drawing God into the center of your body.
- Be aware that you are breathing in the power and presence of God each time you breathe in. Stay with the awareness for a while.
- Then imagine that you are breathing out all of your impurities, your fears, resentments, self-sufficiency, and anger.
- Follow this with a heart-to-heart conversation with God.

Chapter 3

Deciding to "Go Steady"

Practicing the Presence of God

*Our pursuit of God is successful because He is forever seeking to
manifest Himself to us.*

A. W. TOZER

*We are put on this earth for a little space
That we may learn to bear the beams of Love.*

WILLIAM BLAKE

*Taste and see that the LORD is good;
blessed is the man who takes refuge in him.*

PSALM 34:8

Carolyn Gratton opens her book *The Art of Spiritual Guidance* with this
story:

It seems that there once were some fish who spent their days swimming
around in search of water. Anxiously looking for their destination, they
shared their worries and confusion with each other as they swam. One
day they met a wise fish and asked him the question that had preoccupied them for so long: "Where is the sea?" The wise fish answered: "If

you stop swimming so busily and struggling so anxiously, you would discover that you are already in the sea. You need look no further than where you already are."[1]

For Gratton the wise fish represents a spiritual director that is in touch with the omnipresence of God. The search for water represents our search for life in the kingdom. Hurry depicts the devil.

As I type these words I recall hearing on the radio about a church that was sponsoring a special service. The minister of music was being touted as a reason to attend. "Come on out this Sunday evening, John Smith [not his real name; his real name was John Doe] will be singing and leading the worship service. He can really lead you into the presence of the Lord."

I thought then, as I do now, that the real trick would be finding someone who could lead you *out* of God's omnipresence. We exist in the loving ocean of God's being. We cannot attain the company of God. What may be missing, however, is our awareness of his transforming presence and a trust that the environment is friendly. Mystics and poets already know this. They are the wise fish. To become like them, we must recognize that God is not "up there" somewhere; he is right here and right now. We must show up and participate in the relationship, and we must rid ourselves of those things that keep us from him.

GOD DESIRES TO BE WITH US

God declares his desire for us to enjoy his presence on a boldfaced billboard visible from most any location across the landscape of Scripture. Step inside the Bible anywhere between "In the beginning" (Genesis 1:1) and "Amen" (Revelation 22:21) and glance around. We don't have to look very far before we bump into one of four themes—inheritance, presence, rejection, grace—each of which relates to God's presence and desire for relationship with those he crafted.

First, *God has prepared a suitable dwelling place for his people* both as an inheritance and as a place for being together. Initially, he created that famous garden. After Adam and Eve rejected it, God prepared another dwelling place, the Promised Land, a communal table set with condiments of milk and honey. When we pushed away that inheritance, he sent his Son with the deed to yet another, the kingdom of heaven.

Second, *God desires to be with his people in loving relationship.* He was present with Adam and Eve in the garden, walking and talking with them in the cool of day. After they left home, he again offered his presence in the Holy of Holies, the central part of the tabernacle in the wilderness and later the temple in Jerusalem.

When we turned this place, which was designed for conversation and communion, into a supermarket of grasping and hiding, God sent his Son through the mystery of incarnation to be *with* us. Christ completed his mission of presence but even then refused to leave us alone. Next he sent his own Spirit to dwell *within* the Holy of Holies of any believer who would put out a welcome

St. Theophan the Recluse

Everywhere and always God is with us, near to us and in us. But we are not always with Him, since we do not remember Him; and because we do not remember Him we allow ourselves many things which we would not permit if we did remember. Take upon yourself this task—to make a habit of such recollection. Make yourself a rule always to be with the Lord, keeping your mind in your heart, and do not let your thoughts wander; as often as they stray, turn them back again and keep them at home in the closet of your heart, and delight in converse with the Lord.[2]

mat. And through the two millenniums of church history the sacrament of the Eucharist (Christ within) became a concrete picture and the mystical reality of abiding presence.

Third, *humanity continually rejects both the inheritance and the offer of presence and relationship.* Like a teenager obsessed with independence, like the prodigal son headed east, the created continue to leave home to live on our own. Then it was behind a bush in paradise; now it's behind a desk in a lonely corporate office or a kitchen sink in a subdivision. With tear-streaked cheeks we come to realize the cost of autonomy. The price of independence from God is the deep ache of loneliness.

But all is not lost. This is the fourth theme. Thank God, *he does not give up on us.* When we rejected the Old Covenant, God crafted a new one. When we ridiculed the prophets, God sent his own Son. And even after humanity murdered Christ, God's love and desire for intimate communion did not waiver. *He never lets go of his desire for relationship,* sending his Spirit to find us, offer us counsel, and dwell within us. We become the temple of his presence, our hearts the new Holy of Holies.

The four uniting themes of Scripture—inheritance, presence, rejection, grace—reveal God's passion to be with us as a healing presence of love. But to enjoy our relationship with him, we must be fully present to it. We must participate in it. The following story illustrates what this means and why it's so critical.

PARTICIPATING IN THE RELATIONSHIP

My good friend Tim fell deeply in love not long after his first pimple popped out and said hey. He was thirteen years old and in the eighth grade. The object of his affection was a seventh grader named Jill who attended the same middle school. She had straight blonde hair, deep blue eyes, and liked to wear cardigan sweaters with a gold clasp at the top.

Even though Jill lived in Tim's neighborhood and was the younger sister of his best friend, Mike, Tim hadn't really noticed her until she walked past him in the hallway one day. Something was different about Jill. Perhaps it was the sweater.

Before you could say "puppy love," all the love songs on the radio suddenly made sense. Tim spent the rest of his eighth-grade year finding reasons to pass Jill in the hallway, each time hoping to collect the courage to ask her *the* question.

The last day of school was his final chance to see her on a daily basis. So he sucked in some air, threw his shoulders back, and did the manly thing. He pretended to bump into Jill as she was taking books from her locker.

"Oh, excuse me. Sorry. Uh, well, I was thinking, is that a new sweater? No, I mean. Do you think you might want to go together this summer?"

She blushed and said yes.

Barry Manilow sang in Tim's head as he raced off to class.

For the first few weeks of the summer he wasn't himself. His ravenous appetite had been replaced by canary-sized cravings, and his obsession with sports had been bumped by a single-minded focus on Jill. Would she prefer candy or flowers? Was she thinking about him in that exact same moment?

Tim became so infatuated that he began to worry, *What if she changes her mind? What if she wants to quit going with me?*

Fear began to wrestle with love in his mind. *If she doesn't want to go with me, that would be worse than death,* he reasoned and became increasingly worried.

Tim quit going to Mike's house as much as he used to. And when he was there, and saw Jill, he would just stick up his hand, say hi, and quickly look away. Sometimes, not wanting to appear desperate, he even tried to ignore her. Going with her was just too important to risk doing something stupid that would mess it up.

Just before summer ended, Tim asked Mike to deliver a note to his sister. On it he wrote, "Dear Jill. Are we still going together?"

Her reply, delivered through the voice of her brother, broke his young heart.

She said, "Not anymore, since we never actually went anywhere."

Tim's all grown up now. He recovered nicely and managed to find himself a wife and two children along the way.

He told me that story because I was telling him about the idea behind this book—that developing a transforming relationship with God is a lot like developing a relationship with a spouse, each requiring a lot of time for conversation, communion, and union.

Tim told me that made him think about his experience with Jill, and he said that wasn't the only time he had let fear keep him from doing the most important thing in a relationship: showing up and being fully present. He said that most of the time he handles his relationship with God the same way—even now, as a pastor. Avoiding God's presence for fear of rejection but all the while hoping that they are still going together.

"But there is one difference," I heard myself say. "God is everywhere. He is always with us—it's just that we don't always choose to participate in the relationship."

Do you ever feel like Tim when it comes to going with God? Do you ever get a little nervous and avoid showing up, tuning in? I have. I know God loves me. I've seen it in writing and even heard him whisper it to me. But there have been prolonged times when, except for occasionally catching a glimpse of him in his house, I didn't see God much, and I didn't seek him out. What's up with that?

Well, for me, when it's just a matter of discipline or focus, the following ideas have been helpful:

1. Consider that the word *heaven* does not refer to a realm out there somewhere but rather to the air that surrounds you. You are already engulfed within the heavens. I like to reflect on this while slowly praying the first line of the Lord's Prayer, "Our Father which art in heaven." To do this frequently helps me to consider the mystery of God's presence.

2. Allow each time you look at your watch or calendar to be a prompt to think about God's presence with you.

3. Let your breathing symbolize a form of communion with God. Take a few minutes to slow down and breathe deeply. As you inhale, pray: *Lord, Jesus, please be present in every cell of my body.* And as you exhale, pray: *Take away my fears and anxiety.*

4. Develop the habit of returning to an awareness of God's presence in the midst of daily tasks. For instance:
   - Allow every red light or stop sign to be an occasion for a deep breath and a conversation with God.
   - Every time you take a drink, think to yourself, *God, you too are present all around and in the very center of my being.*
   - When you are talking with a friend, visualize the mystery of God's presence in him. Notice how it changes the interaction. (But don't worship your friend, or you've taken this too far.)
   - Whenever you are driving and the passenger seat is empty, imagine that Jesus is sitting beside you and strike up a conversation.
   - Before getting out of bed each morning, say in an audible voice, "God, this day is yours. Please help me to tune in to your presence as we walk through it together."

5. As you go through the day, frequently announce to God, "Here I am. What would you like to do next?"

6. At the end of the day, thank God for his presence with you, and let him know you are looking forward to spending the whole day with him again tomorrow.

If God has seemed to be in a galaxy far, far away, the above list may be all you need to begin cultivating an awareness of his presence and enjoying him more. But for some, missing out on a perpetual awareness of God's presence is a much deeper problem than the need to tie a string around their finger so that they show up.

GOING DEEPER

Most of us approach God in one of two ways: religion or righteousness. In fact, the distinction between these two approaches defines how we will experience God. The difference between them has everything to do with the presence or absence of deep, personal affection.[3]

During Jesus' time on earth, religious people seemed to get on his nerves. But he loved to lavish time on the righteous. Why?

The word *religion* comes from the Latin word *ligare,* which refers to something binding an individual, as a "ligament" binds muscle to bone. The Pharisees were religious. They were bound to the law, and they tried to obligate God to offer acceptance and reward with their scrupulous compliance to it. Control interested them more than compassion, rules more than relationship.

Religion always degenerates into a human-crafted scheming to influence divinity. Religion is whatever you and I do in order to get God to love us more than we think he would be spontaneously inclined to do. Religion is about control.

Righteousness, as understood in the Old Testament, means something quite different. It is a thoroughly Hebraic concept, mostly foreign to the Western mind.[4] Righteousness connotes a relationship characterized by mutual delight in one another, and by loyalty, esteem, and lasting commitment. In a righteous relationship, love defines right behavior toward the other. Righteousness is about surrender.

Here's another way of contrasting religion and righteousness. Joyfully planning a wedding anniversary getaway with your spouse is righteous activity. Washing dishes to get sex is a religious act.

Religious people fear God and look for ways to keep him at a distance and to bind his wrath. They turn their affections primarily inward. But righteous people love God and look for ways to enjoy his presence.

Does this sound appealing—to untie the fetters of religious control so that you can be free to enjoy and mutually delight in your fellowship with God? If so, keep reading.

Listen to what A. W. Tozer had to say about why we avoid God's presence.

> We sense that the call is for us [to come into God's presence], but we fail to draw near.... There is something more serious than coldness of heart.... What is it? What but the presence of a veil in our hearts? A veil which remains there still shutting out the light and hiding the face of God from us.... It is the close-woven veil of the self-life which we have never really acknowledged, or of which we have been secretly ashamed.... It is not a thing about which we commonly talk...an enemy to our lives and effective block to the spiritual progress.[5]

What "veils" can cloak our awareness of God's omnipresence? In order to become "wise fish," we must rip down every veil that "hides the face of God from us."

Let's examine three things that commonly keep us from enjoying God's presence and what we can do to be rid of them. The first two have to do with the relationship killers of grasping and hiding, which were briefly introduced in the last chapter. The third relates to our tendency to place the head of one of our parents onto the shoulders of God.

LET GO OF MY FALSE SECURITIES

Before we can let go of false securities—our desire for control rather than surrender—we need to know where they come from. Fear and love are the warp and woof of the universe. They are also opposites, both physiologically *and* spiritually. Neither can be fully alive in the presence of the other. They are emotional oil and water. Fear defines the nature of our false self and motivates religiosity; love is another name for our truest self. Love opens the door to righteousness.

When we are afraid, our body engages in some predictable activities. Our breathing becomes shallow and rapid, our pupils dilate, our heartbeat increases, and our blood pressure rises. Blood moves from the extremities to the major muscles. Sugar dumps into the bloodstream. Fear makes us ready to flee or fight, assault or withdraw.

Love—as well as laughter and relaxation—causes the opposite responses. For a person in love, breathing becomes slow, deep, and diaphragmatic; pupils constrict; heartbeat slows; and blood pressure lowers. Blood moves to the extremities, causing a feeling of warmth and heaviness in the hands and feet. Whereas fear mobilizes us for action, love makes us ready to stay and relate, affirm and move toward.

No sane person likes to experience fear. When afraid, we see ourselves as the threatened center of a hostile universe. We cling to who we are and what we have and desperately look for a solution, something that will remove the threat and turn off our sympathetic nervous system.

It is rare, though, when the problem that flips our switch is a tangible snake or tiger. Most often what frightens us are ephemeral monsters—threats to our need to feel significant, important, valued, and loved, such as getting passed over for a promotion, feeling taken for granted by our spouse, or having a child who no longer comes to us for advice. Events like these threaten our desire to be the center of the universe.

When these fears arise within us, we naturally flee to the shallow surface of our lives instead of descending to the center, where we will find security and the comforting arms of God. We want to reverse the situation, we want to be in control.

Fear can make us forget our true identity as an image, likeness, and child of God. Most of us live in fear. Most of us cling to solutions that are not God, and these false securities keep us from experiencing God himself. God told Moses to throw down his rod (see Exodus 4:3), a symbol of personal power and sufficiency, because he wanted to reveal its true nature. Trusting anything more than God turns the object of our trust into a serpent.

Our use of God-substitutes does more than knock out fear; it begins a process that spirals us away from God's loving presence.

COME OUT OF HIDING

Our own plan for fear management is not the only thing that keeps us behind the veil. We also have a tendency to hide from the divine presence—just like our foreparents.

> Then the man and his wife heard the sound of the LORD God as he
> was walking in the garden in the cool of the day, and they hid from
> the LORD God among the trees of the garden. But the LORD God called
> to the man, "Where are you?"
>
> He answered, "I heard you in the garden, and I was afraid because
> I was naked; so I hid." (Genesis 3:8-10)

Once the serpent planted the seed of worry, it was easy to cause Adam and Eve to grasp at God-substitutes and eat from the tree of self-deification. Their shame over their disobedience caused them to hide, to move away from God's presence and from relationship with him.

Shame raises the veil. Even within the best moments of my marriage, I fear not being accepted. Do I really want another being to experience my morning breath and daily constitutionals? No. I want to be in control of what, when, and how I present myself to another. I only want another to be present when I'm at my best and certain that I will be accepted.

While I don't think that much about God being put off by my halitosis, I do stink, spiritually speaking, many other times each day and prefer not to be reminded of his omnipresence. My false self fears that God will reject me if he sees how poorly I'm imitating his Son and suggests that I move away from awareness of his presence and hide out in my shame. Maybe I'll come out of hiding after I've done more to improve my appearance.

I hide from the awareness of God's presence after I have blown my horn at slow drivers—fast ones too—and choose not to think about him for hours. I retreat from awareness of him after being too busy to keep our morning appointment for a talk yet still managing to check in with the sports pages. When I lose my temper and snap at my daughter, I'd just as soon God be in a galaxy far, far way. I'll let him know when I am ready to reenter his presence.

Far and away the primary cause of my shame is when I, like Adam and Eve, have given God a vote of no confidence and then come to my senses. I am most embarrassed after awakening to the fact that once again I chose my way instead of his. Again and again I have shouted in his face, "I know how to run my life better than you." What statement from a child could cause more injury to a parent? How can I remain in God's presence after doing something so vile?

Yes!. Have you been there? Have you caught yourself in the act of playing God over your life? Were you able to resist taking the same route as Adam and Eve, hiding from God's presence in shame? *not really - but getting better*

It gets pretty crowded in the bushes. So how do we come out of hiding after we realize yet again that we've eaten from the wrong tree?

The answer is almost too simple, too obvious to believe. We step out from behind the veil as we realize that God is not created in our image, we are created in his. Whereas our human response to rejection is anger and punishment, God doesn't respond that way. That is not God's nature. We come out of hiding as we begin to fathom God's intention and true nature. There is no bottom to his love, no boundary to his acceptance. As the truth of this sinks in, the veil becomes thinner and thinner, and the light begins to pour in. *good!*

Still feel sheepish!

RECOGNIZE GOD'S TRUE NATURE

Both our desire for God-substitutes and our shame have a common ground—misperception of God's nature. When we finally come to see God as the prodigal's father, our hands relax their grip, and we come out of hiding. But this isn't easy to do. Let me tell you an inspirational story about a person who came to see God correctly after fifty years of misperceiving. (!)

Susan (not her real name) grew up trying to please a distant and demanding father. No matter what she did—straight A's, perfect attendance in Sunday school, fetching his slippers after work—it was not good enough to earn his approval. Susan's younger sister got what little love their father had, as if his love and acceptance were in limited supply.

It wasn't long until Susan performed the most common spiritual surgery in the universe. She put the head of her earthly father on the shoulders of God. She came to view God as cold, aloof, distant, and demanding—having love for some but not all, certainly not for her.

Yet she didn't give up. She kept trying to win the attention of both her fathers, trying desperately to be the perfect child, young lady, and finally, adult. It was exhausting.

Then one weekend, while on a spiritual retreat, she was asked to draw a picture of God. It was easy. She just closed her eyes and there he was, holding a ruler over her head with a look that said, you just don't measure up. She drew herself with sad eyes and looking up at an impossible-to-please God.

Later, with encouragement to talk with God in prayer about her view of him, a movie began to play in her head. She thinks he turned on the projector.

In the flickering imagery she saw herself standing in a graduation line. She was first in line because she was the valedictorian. She looked around for her father. To her surprise he was present. He was even smiling. *Finally,* she thought, *I've won his approval. Maybe he's even thinking, That's my daughter.*

But then the scene changed. She had been transported to the back of the line. Last in her class. She felt ashamed and alone. When the time finally came for her to cross the stage and get her diploma, she looked out into the audience and saw a surprising sight. There was God, smiling and waving and shouting, "That's my girl. I'm so proud of you!"

In the "dream" she walked back to her seat. But before she could sit down, God grabbed her cap with great excitement and sailed it into the air. His love for her was astounding.

When Susan asked God for a review of the movie he had just directed in her head, she sensed the meaning. He wanted her to know that her images of him were all wrong. He was not cold, distant, or demanding. He loved her, accepted her, and only wanted to see her filled with joy, dancing with joy.

"In a moment," Susan says, "my view of God changed, and I knew I had been seeing him as a reflection of my father. God is not my earthly father. He's not some impossible-to-please shop foreman who only cares about what I can produce. He's my friend and my dance partner. He's asked me to dance, and I've said yes."

And in that next moment, Susan was able to let go of a false picture of God and her need to be perfect in hope of winning approval. She came out of hiding and let go of her grasp on perfectionism. She became open and receptive to her heavenly Father's presence and began with him a journey of conversation, communion, and consummation. She discovered the sea that had always engulfed her.

Our ideas and images of God are of supreme importance. From the first temptation in the garden to our most recent, Satan strategizes to implant in us false pictures of God, pictures that would make us run away from him instead of toward him.

While it comes in many shades and hues, the primary corrupt view is that God cannot be trusted with our life, and therefore we must act on our own. We must grasp. And after grasping, we hide. Both acts take us away from relationship, away from love. To once again quote A. W. Tozer,

A right conception of God is basic not only to systematic theology but to practical Christian living as well. It is to worship what the foundation is to the temple; where it is inadequate or out of plumb the whole structure must sooner or later collapse. I believe there is scarcely an error in doctrine or a failure in applying Christian ethics that cannot be traced finally to imperfect and ignoble thoughts about God.[6]

Susan imagined God to be just like her father—cold, distant, and aloof—and consequently avoided being vulnerable and real in his presence. She exhausted herself trying to earn his love. Religion did not work, and the veil of separation was thick.

When God could stand it no more, he shattered her graven images and replaced them with a clearer picture of him. Then he tore through the veil of separation and began to establish a healing relationship with his precious child.

GOING WITH GOD

One of history's most notable figures that decided to *go with* God was Nicholas Herman, better known as Brother Lawrence. His education was minimal, his career was primarily confined to kitchen work, he had dishpan hands, and his existence was pretty much unremarkable—except for one thing. He made his life a grand experiment for living every moment in awareness of the presence of God.

In the words of Richard J. Foster, "His attempts to create an habitual state of communion led to new heights of spiritual living."[7] Brother Lawrence became a pioneer who discovered a new world—the kingdom of God—and inspired others to travel there as well.

In addition to his profound discipline and desire, Brother Lawrence was able to "image" God properly, as a king, full of mercy and goodness. Listen to his description of how he saw himself in God's presence and how he viewed God.

> I image myself as the most wretched of all, full of sores and sins, and one who had committed all sorts of crimes against his king. Feeling deep sorrow, I confess to him all of my sins, I ask him for forgiveness, and I abandon myself into his hands so that he may do with me what he pleases.
>
> The king, full of mercy and goodness, very far from chastening me, embraces me with love, invites me to feast at his table, serves me with his own hands, and gives me the key to his treasures. He converses with me, and takes delight in me, and treats me as if I were his favorite. This is how I imagine myself from time to time in his holy presence.[8]

Yes, this view of God can inspire us to take the time to go with him, to let go of false securities, and to come out of hiding. That is the view—divine goodness and mercy—that moves us into deeper awareness of his presence and inspires healing conversation and deeper levels of communion.

That Brother Lawrence, he was one wise fish.

~~~

Bible Study: Jesus Practiced What He Preached

Text: Mark 1:29-39; 15:37-39

> As soon as they left the synagogue, they went with James and John to the home of Simon and Andrew. Simon's mother-in-law was in bed

with a fever, and they told Jesus about her. So he went to her, took her hand and helped her up. The fever left her and she began to wait on them.

That evening after sunset the people brought to Jesus all the sick and demon-possessed. The whole town gathered at the door, and Jesus healed many who had various diseases. He also drove out many demons, but he would not let the demons speak because they knew who he was.

Very early in the morning, while it was still dark, Jesus got up, left the house and went off to a solitary place, where he prayed. Simon and his companions went to look for him, and when they found him, they exclaimed: "Everyone is looking for you!"

Jesus replied, "Let us go somewhere else—to the nearby villages—so I can preach there also. That is why I have come." So he traveled throughout Galilee, preaching in their synagogues and driving out demons.

With a loud cry, Jesus breathed his last.

The curtain of the temple was torn in two from top to bottom. And when the centurion, who stood there in front of Jesus, heard his cry and saw how he died, he said, "Surely this man was the Son of God!"

Observations

Consider this story from the perspective of Peter's mother-in-law. Her precious daughter does not marry a doctor, lawyer, or even that tax collector, Matthew. She marries a fisherman. Seasonal work. Fish guts to the elbows. Coming home with a stench that would distract a leper. Not the best of jobs, but at least it is a job.

Then along comes a carpenter's son from a town even smaller than Capernaum. Everyone knows nothing good can ever come out of that one-camel town. What's this, is Peter crazy? He's the sole provider for that precious child. He turned in his nets and became unemployed. He gave away his boat—filled with fish! This Jesus is a bad influence. He's got to be put in his place.

But then she gets sick. Real sick. She lies on her bed in a cold sweat. No insurance. No husband. No gainfully employed son-in-law.

Jesus appears in her doorway. Stands over her bed. The troublemaker. The bad influence. She wants to give him a piece of her fevered mind. But look at him. Those eyes. So kind. His touch. Gentle. Real. His touch. It draws her fever away, like fatback pulling out a splinter.[9] Her fever fades, and health comes gushing in and paints her cheeks. Jesus! Maybe he isn't such a bum. Peter's mother-in-law, with her renewed strength, rises from bed and begins to prepare dinner for Jesus and Peter and his friends.

After the meal, the whole town turns out. Doctors, lawyers, tax collectors, the sick, the outcasts, and the demon-possessed. Jesus wades into the crowd. What he did for her, he does for them all. Fevers stop boiling. Sores disappear. Demons are sent packing. Wow! That Peter is one precocious son-in-law.

But the next morning Peter can't find Jesus—just when he is hoping Jesus will put in a good word with his mother-in-law. Where is he?

Long before the first cock crowed, Jesus had arisen and gone off to a solitary place. He wanted to be alone with his Father. He wanted to be in his presence, hear his voice.

Hours pass before Peter and his friends catch up with Jesus.

"Let's go back, Jesus. You were right. It has begun. Let's get a tent and hire an organist. It's begun."

But Jesus does not listen. He doesn't go back to the site of the revival. He tells them it's time to move on.

How does he know that? What gives him the fortitude to leave a sure thing and set sail for the uncertain?

The secret, according to Henri Nouwen, is found in the solitary place.

That is where Jesus meets with his Father. Alone in an ocean of love. That is where he enjoys God's presence and receives direction.

When Jesus dies, the veil in the temple is torn top to bottom, a signal that the secret of Jesus' ministry is now available to all. The presence of God. No veils. Just God.

Reflection Questions

1. What do you think Nouwen meant when he said, "The secret of Jesus' ministry is hidden in [solitude]"[10]?
2. The first thing Mark recorded in his gospel after the death of Jesus was the tearing of the veil in the temple. What are the implications of this for you?
3. How might the discipline of solitude (removing yourself from the noise and distractions of the world for a period of time) relate to practicing the presence of God?
4. Describe your most real awareness of God's presence during a time when you practiced solitude.

Meditation: God Views

Explanation

"Tell me a person's view of God and I'll tell you how he lives his life." That's what comedian Curt Cloninger often says before performing his drama titled *God Views*. It's a powerful theater piece inspired by J. B. Phillips's classic, *Your God Is Too Small.*

In the performance, Curt portrays six false views of God that plague the imagination of so many. God is seen as a cosmic sheriff, senile grandfather, production-minded shop foreman, waiter, party host, and a weak god-in-a-box. Needless to say, each image is not one you would want to "go with."

He then provides a powerful, modern-day reenactment of the story of the prodigal son. God is seen as the prodigal's father, brimming with mercy and goodness. It's the animated picture of healing presence. It's an image of God that draws you near.

Exercise

Take a few moments and look back over the course of your life—preschool days, elementary school, middle and high school memories, all the way forward to the present. Consider the most heretical view of God you've ever had—perhaps it haunts you now. How did you picture him? How would you capture it on paper?

Then consider the most true and accurate picture of God that has ever been drawn in your imagination. How would you draw it on paper?

Meditation

With both views of God in mind and perhaps actually on paper, take a few moments to quiet yourself. Allow yourself to become aware of God's presence. Imagine the ocean of grace that surrounds you.

Then offer him the false picture of himself. See yourself as a small child handing a drawing to him. Let it go. Leave it with him.

Then describe to God the other picture—the one you believe best captures his presence in your life. Then ask God to draw a picture of himself for you. Ask him to explain what he drew and if you can have the copy.

Spiritual Exercise: The Empty Chair

A Final Reminder

Begin by taking five to ten minutes to monitor and experience the Five Ps of Prayer.

The Empty Chair

Place an empty chair next to you in an ideal location for conversing with a friend.

Take five to ten minutes to quiet yourself with those Five Ps of Prayer.

Then imagine Jesus present in the chair that is facing you. Slowly study him with the five senses of your imagination. Pay particular attention to how he looks, the expression on his face, his eyes.

Continue to view him as you initiate a conversation.

Chapter 4

Learning to Listen

How to Hear God's Voice

> *I keep myself by a simple attention and a general fond regard to God, which I refer to as an actual presence of God. Or, to put it another way, an habitual, silent, and secret conversation of the soul with God.*
>
> BROTHER LAWRENCE

> *I believe the most adequate description of prayer is simply talking to God about what we are doing together.*
>
> *Human beings were once alive to God. They were created to be responsive to and interactive with him. Adam and Eve lived in conversational relationship with their creator, daily renewed. When they mistrusted God and disobeyed him that cut them off from the realm of the Spirit. They became as dead to the realm of the Spirit as a kitten is dead to arithmetic.*
>
> DALLAS WILLARD

At this moment more than one hundred transmissions are bouncing off my body, and that's just from the basic Dish Network package. DirecTV, satellite radio, and at least one local AM station also saturate the room where I sit. But none of this affects me; I'm not tuned in. Most of us live in God's kingdom in a similar way. Most of us are unaware of all the invisible activity or that God is speaking to us.

Yet God has created us for intimate friendship with himself.[1] We are his children, encouraged to call him Daddy. We are designed to live with him in an ongoing conversation, daily renewed. God would routinely visit with us as he did with Eve, Enoch, David, and Christ incarnate.

But we have a problem. We can't live as we were created to live. We have tumbled from God's expansive kingdom into our own cramped fiefdoms. We are not attuned to his presence. We don't even have satellite receivers, unless we've asked him to do the installation. And even if we have a dish installed, even if we awake to the existence of a communicating King, we still face the dilemma of discerning which broadcasts are from him.

I have found help for hearing God's voice and distinguishing between those voices that come from him and those that come from others or even me by:

- shutting up (practicing the discipline of silence)
- staying close (making use of solitude)
- differentiating his voice from other voices (practical discernment)

Who says kittens can't learn to multiply?

SHUT UP SO THE COACH CAN SPEAK

I've spent the past fifteen years training counselors, and since 90 percent of what these helpers do is listen, they need to learn to shut up. If we want to communicate with God, we will do the same.

This concept sounds simple, but most of us spend most of our time with God talking to him, not listening to see if he has something to say to us. No wonder we never hear him say anything. He can't get a word in edgewise! I'm a slow learner, and I didn't see this problem in my own life until I was coaching my daughter's basketball team. Let me explain.

Basketball Diaries

Being a frustrated athlete, I was delighted when I noticed that Jesse, our first-born, was the tallest kid in her third-grade class. I was almost giddy when she announced she would like to play basketball. Before the sun set on her procla-mation, I had her signed up with the local recreation league. The team draft would be in two days.

Forty-eight hours isn't much time to turn a kid who had never said hello to a basketball into Michelle Jordan, but I tried. A crash camp of driveway dribbling, two-hand chest passes, and grabbing rebounds as they bounced off our roof was put in place.

I took Jesse to tryouts, and after supper that evening the phone rang. She'd made the team! Even better, they asked me to be the coach. How did they know that was my other unfulfilled fantasy? Not only had they recognized my daughter's talent, somehow they had detected my untapped potential to draw Xs and Os.

I scheduled a team practice for the next night. Three kids on the team (my daughter being one) had potential, but it was obvious that each was new to the sport of basketball. My other four players were the most hyperactive crew I had ever witnessed—and I was a practicing psychologist at the time. Hands, feet, and mouths a-blur. They were chaos on steroids, frenzy doing speed.

When the first game rolled around, we lost 44–0.

Later that night the truth hit me like a flagrant foul. My team was com-posed of the seven kids that none of the other coaches had picked, and I was the hypereager sucker selected to be their coach. We were in big trouble.

At some dark moment between our first and second games, I was driving with the radio on and heard an announcement about a contest—perhaps they were giving away free towels. While we didn't particularly need towels, the notion of winning something set my mind to working. I knew very well what I would like to win.

I dreamed of a contest where I could win time with a top basketball coach—

like Phil Jackson. Yes, every morning at 7:00 a.m. Phil would arrive by helicopter. I would greet him at the door, and then we would sit in our living room. For as long as I liked, I could ask him questions about basketball, get advice on Xs and Os, and find out where he bought his suits and if they came in normal sizes.

But then it hit me. *I've already won a far better contest than that.* And so have you! The Creator of Life has made himself available to me twenty-four hours a day, every day of my life. I can sit with him in my living room or talk to him while standing in line at Wal-Mart. I've already won access to the greatest coach in the universe!

But what if I never sit down with him? Or even if I do, what if I never ask him any questions or engage him in conversation. *What if I do all the talking?* Well, when it came to how I had spent my time with God, that's exactly what I had been doing my whole life. I had made prayer a monologue.

For more than thirty years I had access to the ultimate coach in the universe, but the communication was always only one way. I never engaged him in dialogue. I droned on and on about what I wanted him to do or why he should like me, but *I never shut up and listened to the coach!*

Silence is the most foundational of all Christian disciplines. Silence minimizes any distractions so that we will be better able to hear. While it involves reduction of noise and speech, it always involves the act of listening. Through the centuries devotion masters have written about the importance of inner quietness and holy receptivity.

I love to visit monasteries, but my affection increased with my new desire to actually hear from the coach. My favorite monastery is home for a Trappist community just outside of Atlanta. The next time I went there for a retreat, I was all ears.

I turned onto the grounds and drove down a long, tree-lined driveway, making a conscious act of switching off the car radio to better tune in to WGOD. Silence engulfed me. Dried magnolia leaves crunched as my tires rolled over them. A monk wearing black and white walked by the road, appearing lost in prayer. I remember hoping the leaves did not disturb him. Prompted by speed bumps, I slowed the car and my thoughts even more.

Inside the monastery, I unpacked a few things in a small cell that would make a room at the Motel 6 look like a suite. I was aware of the smooth noise of sliding wooden drawers and the flutter of a bird outside. I walked to the church and noticed how much sound was coming from my leather shoes as they hit the stone floor. I sat in a wooden pew and listened. I could hear my breathing as air slowly escaped through my nose. After a few minutes I became aware of the pulse in my ears. My jaw relaxed and fell open. The silence began to sound like the inside of a seashell.

In the holy hush I also started to notice other things that had escaped my attention. I became inspired by the smell of candles and the warm lighting of the room through stained-glass windows. My thoughts became even slower, so slow and unobtrusive that I became keenly aware of God's presence. I sensed he wanted to talk and that he'd been anticipating our time together.

I wanted to ask for dozens of things: good health for my family, career success, a better relationship with my wife, more time with my daughters, but I said nothing. Instead, I listened.

After a while I heard something that stilled the wind behind all my questions. *I love you,* he said. *I love you even more than you love your children. And I will love you and take care of you forever. Let's just enjoy being together.*

God's words are worth millions of ours. How important it is for us to listen to the Author of Life. Those times that we do, we experience what our promises and productivity cannot buy. In silence—which is more about listening than the absence of noise—we are better able to hear what is truly important.

STAY CLOSE TO THE ONE YOU WANT TO HEAR

If we want to hear God's voice, we will do more than shut up and listen. We will also stay close to the One we want to hear. For most of us, this amounts to a major change in how we live our lives. No wonder it's so tempting to play Bible roulette instead.

Have you ever played Bible roulette? You know, you're faced with a difficult issue in your life. Where should I go to college? How long should I keep working this dead-end job? Is it time to start a family? Will my son be healed of diabetes? Desperate to hear from God, you spot it, his Book, lying on a table.

You pick it up and place it vertically between your hands. "God," you whisper, "please guide me through your written Word to your will for me."

Ways to Stay Close to God and Develop Our Hearing

1. Wake up and greet God with a warm "good morning," and listen for his response.
2. Read favorite portions of Scripture as faded love letters — listening for the voice of the author as you read.
3. Recognize the long line at the grocery as an opportunity for a few deep breaths and a time to listen for the voice of God.
4. Make sure your day planner has at least one appointment with God that is written in indelible ink. Close the door. Offer him an empty chair. Then…shut up, be patient, and lean in.
5. See each person you meet as a new opportunity to show love to the *imago dei* (the image of God buried inside him). God's reflection is on every face.
6. Hugging your spouse or children can become a sacrament of communicating love to God.
7. When you turn the light off, ask God if he enjoyed spending the day together and listen for his response.

You let the big, black Book fall open between your hands.

No, you think, *I caused that with my thumbnail. Better do that again.*

Second try. The Bible opens and the ball drops. Second Peter 2:22: "Of them the proverbs are true: 'A dog returns to its vomit,' and, 'A sow that is washed goes back to her wallowing in the mud.'"

What does that mean, God? What are you trying to say?

The answer to both questions is probably "nothing." Or better yet, "If you want quick answers, call a 900 number. What I want is to develop a relationship with you that will be constant, intimate, conversational, and transforming."

Intimate relationship and transforming dialogue can't be rushed.

Other hurried approaches to hearing from God may include: Sunday-morning-only requests; asking questions just when in trouble; and asking someone "more religious" to get a "word" on our behalf.

But God is not interested in our games and superstitions. The "right answer" is not the answer. He is the answer. Daily renewed relationship is the Holy Grail from which he wants us to drink. We must desire to be with him. We must desire his *presence* more than his *presents.*

Discerning the sound of God's voice requires an overall approach to life in which we organize our days around staying close to him. If you want to hear the flutes, you'd better sit on the front row.

Max Lucado beautifully summarizes this point in a story he penned in *Tell Me the Secrets: Treasures for Eternity.* In the fable, three knights face the task of navigating a dark forest populated by clever, yellow-eyed creatures that stand in their way. The reward for the first knight to find his way back home—to the castle—is the hand of the king's daughter. Each is allowed one traveling companion.

To help the knights in their journey through the dark forest, the king will play a song on his flute from the castle wall. There are only two flutes. The king has one, and his son, the prince, has the other.

Each knight is known for a particular skill. One is strong. Another swift. The third is wise.

At the end of the story we learn that strength and speed were no match for the wiles of the dark forest and the yellow-eyed creatures who opposed their journey. Only the wise knight survived to claim the hand of the princess. But even he was almost undone by the creatures in the forest who imitated the song of the king.

So how did the wise knight find his way home? He chose the right companion for the journey. He selected the prince to go with him, and as they traveled, the prince played the same song as the king. The wise knight learned it so well that though a thousand false flutes tried to hide the king's music, he could still hear it.

If we are serious about hearing God, we will stay close to him. We will have frequent times where we allow the discipline of silence to deepen into solitude. In solitude—which is more a state of mind than a place—we purposefully withdraw from interaction with others for the purpose of being with God. As Teresa of Avila stated, "Settle yourself in solitude and you will come upon Him in yourself."[2]

Because we specifically enter into solitude for the purpose of being with God, it can become a furnace of transformation. In solitude we begin to recognize the deceitful and imitating voice of our false self as it struggles to move us away from God, and we resist its compulsions to control. In solitude the voice of God becomes true, steady, and inviting, his whispers of love sustenance for our true self.

As referenced in the previous chapter, Jesus knew that the practice of solitude sharpens our awareness of God's presence and helps us learn to recognize God's voice. In the Gospels, Jesus often retreated from people to better discern the will of his Father. He sought solitude:

- by spending forty days in the desert at the beginning of his ministry (see Matthew 4:1-11)
- after his first day of public ministry (see Mark 1:35)
- before choosing the twelve disciples (see Luke 6:12)

- after receiving the news of the death of John the Baptist (see Matthew 14:13)
- after feeding the five thousand (see Matthew 14:23)
- before his transfiguration (see Matthew 17:1-9)
- as he prepared for accepting the cross (see Matthew 26:36-46)

Scripture witnesses that even the Son of God needed to stay close to his Father—especially at times when he needed to receive wisdom and hear a loving voice. Somehow we also know that unless we stay close to God, our lives are in danger.

How Do I Know That Was You, God?

But even when we stay close to God all day, we can still have times when we feel unsure if what we heard reflects the voice of God and not that of the thief and the robber or even our own thoughts. About two decades ago I learned some principles that have helped me have more confidence in my ability to discern whose voice I'm hearing.

My wife and I were conducting an assault on retreat centers. We were taking student sabbaticals, which sounds a lot better than "we had a little money in the bank and decided to put off getting a nine-to-five job until it was all gone."

During that year we visited more than forty spiritual retreat centers in the United States and managed to stay for a while with the world's only collection of Reformed Protestant monks in Taize, France.

About midway through that luxurious year, we found our way to a conference being hosted by Peter Lord at his church in Titusville, Florida.[3] His topic was "Indications of the Voice of God." I had never before—nor have I since—heard a more practical approach to discernment. Following that weekend I began to practice his suggestions during times of listening prayer and to explore what others, from Ignatius of Loyola to obscure prayer warriors, have recommended for discerning the voice of God. I've also had the privilege of teaching these principles to hundreds of students. I would like to share some of these suggestions with you.

But remember, this type of practical discernment is only meant for someone who has already learned to shut up and is attempting to fill each day with little crumbs and bubbles of connectivity to God's kingdom and presence.

Two Radio Stations...Better Make That Three

Imagine that antennae are sticking out of opposite sides of your head, causing you to look like someone from *My Favorite Martian.* One picks up signals from WGOD. That's the soft, melodious FM station that for some reason seems to broadcast with a minimal number of watts. Difficult to tune in but very rewarding when you can pick it up.

Your other antenna points toward WSIN. It's that loud, blaring AM station with more wattage than a thousand laser beams. It's difficult to tune out and very distracting.

Discerning the voice of God has a lot to do with being able to distinguish whether you are listening to WGOD (channel 1) or WSIN (channel 2). Both stations use the speaker system of your thoughts to convert their signals into decipherable receptions.

Another station, WSLF, also plays through your thoughts. It's your own stream of consciousness. But for our purposes here, we will be primarily concerned with distinguishing between WGOD and WSIN. We'll assume signals not easily categorized as channel 1 or 2 are probably very local broadcasts.

Peter Lord suggests the following four categories for distinguishing the voice of God from that of the thief and the robber: nature of the approach, content, relevance of the content, and effects of the content.

Nature of the Approach

Do you remember the children's story about a gullible gingerbread man and a cunning fox? I do. It was my least favorite story when I was a child.

The gingerbread man needs to cross a river but can't do so without getting soggy. A fox sees his predicament and pretends to have the little man's best interests at heart. He persuades the gingerbread man to climb onto his back with solemn assurances that he will not be eaten. But halfway across the river the fox's true nature emerges, and the rest is dessert.

When we understand the nature of God, we are better able to discern his true voice. We don't have to wonder about God's nature. It has been revealed in the person of Jesus Christ. Jesus embodies the nature of his Father. Arguably, the best image we have for Christ is that of a gentle shepherd filled with compassion for his lost sheep. Loving, guarding, inviting, and leading. Just the opposite of a cattle driver: driving, pushing, loud, and aggressive.

The first question I ask myself when trying to discern if what I heard was from channel 1 (WGOD) or 2 (WSIN) is simply this: Was the communication consistent with the quiet leading voice of a shepherd? Or did I feel driven or pushed along by the words? Bottom line: Does what I heard sound like something Jesus would say?

A second point to consider concerning the nature of the approach comes from John 10:1-10. In these verses we learn more about the shepherd and his flock. The shepherd enters the sheep pen by the gate; he calls his sheep by name and leads them out; he goes ahead of them and they follow him because they know his voice.

Jesus is the Good Shepherd. He alone loves with a love so strong that he is willing to lay down his life for the sheep. When invited, he speaks with words best described as loving. By contrast, the thief and robber does not enter by the gate, but makes an illegal entrance, and the sheep do not follow him, because they do not know his voice.

Here's an example of what this means, practically speaking. Let's say you are driving down the road, thinking about your day, and suddenly a thought pops into your head. *You were a jerk last night. You snapped at your wife, didn't kiss your children good night, and went to bed in a huff. You'll be lucky if they don't hate you. And it's your fault.* "What can I do?" you whisper. *Nothing. You'll always be a jerk.*

Before being tortured by that uninvited thought, you can ask yourself two questions: Did that sound like something Jesus would say? And did I invite that input, or did that thought make an illegal entrance into my mind?

These two questions help us discern the nature of the approach. Regardless of whether we acted jerklike, would Jesus, like a cattle driver, snap the whip at us? Would he bound over the wall, uninvited? I think not, and no.

This is not to say we should assume everything that pops into our minds that we haven't been talking to God about is from the devil. It may come from that third broadcasting station, WSLF. And people do suffer with obsessive tendencies. I do mean to say, however, that before allowing a thought to rob us of emotional well-being and before acting on a thought, we should carefully consider the nature of the thought's approach.

If the thought was uninvited and unshepherd-like, the broadcast was not from channel 1.

FROM A CATTLE DRIVER	FROM A SHEPHERD *(Father, is that thought from you?)*
You were a jerk last night.	*No, but I can teach you how to love like I do.*
You snapped at your wife.	*Why don't you call her from work and apologize?*
You didn't kiss your children good night.	*I'll kiss them for you today, and you can give them two tonight.*
They'll hate you.	*I'll teach you to love them with a love that will last for all time.*
It's your fault and there's nothing you can do to change.	*Solutions are so much more important than blame. I'll help you change.*

Content

If there were ever a second invasion of the body snatchers and my wife were stolen and replaced with an exact replica, it would not take me very long to figure out that the person I was talking to was not the real Regina—based on the content of our conversation.

I would ask her, "Do you remember where we went on our tenth wedding anniversary—when we pretended to be rich for a day?" Or I could ask, "Do you remember what you put on Jenna's birthday cake the year she started school?" I could easily distinguish the false from the true by the content of our communication.

When God speaks, the content of the communication will be:

- *In line with scriptural principals.* I believe that Satan, by placing a scriptural address at the end of his communication, deceives many people who are seeking to hear from God. They assume that if a verse is in the mix, it must have come from God. Satan wouldn't quote Scripture. Right? Wrong. We do not have to look past Jesus' trial in the wilderness to see the fallacy here. The devil used Scripture in each of his temptations of Christ. But Jesus realized the error. Satan used proof texts that violated the overall scriptural principal. From the top of the temple in Jerusalem, the devil stood next to Jesus. With a scroll under his arm and a verse in his mouth, the devil quoted from Psalm 91:11-12, "He will command his angels concerning you to guard you in all your ways; they will lift you up in their hands, so that you will not strike your foot against a stone." But Jesus responded with the overall principle that Satan wished to violate: "It is also written: 'Do not put the Lord your God to the test'" (Matthew 4:7, referring to Deuteronomy 6:16). Obscure passages, while still the Word of God, can never bump aside the overarching principles of love, hope, peace, and faith. Simply holding on to the two supreme principles of loving God and your neighbor should be enough to counter the misapplications of Scripture vaulted into your thought life from channel 2.

- *Focused on inner versus outer solutions.* WSIN suggests outer solutions: *Your marriage would be better if your spouse would just see the light and*

Discerning God's Voice—Seven Questions to Ask Yourself[4]

1. *Does it sound like God?* Does what you heard sound like something God would say? Is it consistent with God as you know him through Scripture?

2. *Does it sound like Jesus Christ?* Does it sound like something Jesus would say? Is it consistent with Jesus as you see him revealed in the pages of the New Testament?

3. *Does it help me be conformed to the image of Christ?* The glory of God is our transformation into Christlikeness. (See 2 Corinthians 3:18.)

4. *Is it consistent with a previous experience I have had that I now know was from God?* We can take advantage of the twenty-twenty vision of hindsight.

5. *Is it consistent with the fruit of the Spirit? Does it promote the growth of Christ's character in me?* The fruit of the Spirit is the character of Christ.

6. *Is it consistent with the witness of what the saints and devotion masters have had to say about God?* Do I get a witness from those who have won the race?

7. *Do my closest friends and spiritual mentors believe it was from God?* Do I get a witness from those I trust?

8. *Is it consistent with the overarching themes of Scripture?* God's spoken Word will not contradict his written Word.

---

change or *The church board would be better if so-and-so would resign.* Trouble is, you can do nothing to implement any of these "solutions." Would God recommend an outer solution? Would he frustrate you with advice concerning things you have no power to change? He would not. WGOD gently reminds: *Your marriage will be better when you decide to allow me to love your spouse through you. The church board will be better as you become a better reflection of me [Christ]. Your children will flourish when my loving words flow through your mouth.* Now these are things I can do. These are suggestions for inner solutions.

- *Merciful.* If God had a personal identification card, I'm sure printed on it would be the word *mercy.* That is his nature. God is love. Any communication that is not dripping in mercy is from WSIN. Tune it out.

- *Peacemaking.* Would the Prince of Peace ever suggest fission instead of fusion as a first-line option? No, his first suggestion will always be the clean energy of fusion—putting the unstable back together. If at all possible, we are to avoid the dirty energy of fission, whose effects last for millenniums. WGOD says, *Let me try to help you put that broken relationship back together.* WSIN says, *End your association with that person and never look back.*

- *Correcting instead of condemning.* But what about when I screw up? Does WGOD *only* broadcast forgiveness and grace? WGOD will broadcast *specific conviction* and point out the need for the *correction* of an actual behavior, but rest assured, all broad-sweeping condemnation—especially the condemnation of our personal worth—is from WSIN.

Now for the third category.

Relevance of the Content

Do you believe the devil would ever tell a person to take a trainload of Bibles to northern Siberia? I do. That is, if the communication has the effect of causing the person to begin living in the future, caught up in an impractical, sensational dream instead of being present to the practical and mundane matters of loving those all around.

I know a woman with four wonderful children. But she is hardly aware of their existence. Why? She believes God is calling her to start a ministry among the children in Tanzania. As her own children become dry sponges in need of a few drops of her compassion, I become more convinced that she got that grandiose idea for ministry from WSIN.

WGOD, most typically, broadcasts a simple and definite call for our involvement in the present moment—the marvelously mundane tasks of visiting the sick, baking a cake for a new neighbor, mowing the lawn of an elderly member of our church.

Life is composed of a few billion present moments and nothing more. We are sharing one now as you read this sentence. But now it is gone. Fear not, another present moment is on the horizon. The thief and robber wants to steal life. The easiest way for him to do that is to use thoughts to keep a person tied to the future (even if the focus is ministry) or to the past. But life happens in the present. It is stolen if we are not available to the here and now.

Effects of the Content

The final category for helping us discern if we've heard from God is perhaps the most useful; it has to do with considering the emotional impact of the broadcast. As has often been said, emotions are great servants but terrible masters.

Emotions serve us best as signals to what is going on beneath the surface. For me, anger is a flashing red light that lets me know I have a goal that is being frustrated. Anxiety warns that I'm not trusting God to have my best interests at heart. Depression tells me I've lost something valuable. By contrast, we can typically associate the emotions of love, peace, and joy with a movement toward God, surrender to his kingdom, and the infilling presence of Jesus.

After hearing a broadcast, stop and tune in to the emotions in your body.

Did the communication stir up feelings of love, peace, and joy? Did you feel an increased sense of hope? Was your faith increased? If you can answer yes to any of these questions, there is a great likelihood you heard from channel 1, WGOD.

But, on the other hand, if your emotion meter reads anger, worry, discouragement; if you felt hopelessness, confusion, and deflated faith, the chances are great the broadcast originated from the broadcast tower of WSIN. Ignore the message and change stations.

Of all the principles for discerning God's voice, I have found the best to be the most simple. I am most certain that I have been in dialogue with God when my emotions signal that I am alive with the fruit of Christ's spirit and presence. Those kinds of rewards make me want to shut up and stay close to the King.

HIS EARS ARE JUST FINE

The story is told about an old man who had become concerned about his wife's hearing. He was convinced that she was not too many days removed from being stone deaf. But he could not get her to admit she had a problem and see a doctor.

One day he had had enough and decided to prove his point. He entered their living room where his wife was seated, facing the fireplace. From behind her, he said in a clear voice, "Honey, I love you. Did you hear that?"

No response.

He walked halfway across the room and repeated, "Honey, I said I love you. Do you hear me?"

Nothing.

Finally he walked over, stood in front of her, and shouted, "I love you. Can you hear me now?"

She looked up from her knitting and replied, "Yes, dear, and for the *third* time, I love you too."

Sometimes when I have been talking to God and have come to believe that he has gone deaf, it helps to remember that maybe his ears are just fine. And if I will shut up, stay close, and learn to discard competing broadcasts, I'll hear him say, "I love you too."

~~~

Bible Study: The Shepherd and His Flock

Text: John 10:1-10

"I tell you the truth, the man who does not enter the sheep pen by the gate, but climbs in by some other way, is a thief and a robber. The man who enters by the gate is the shepherd of his sheep. The watchman opens the gate for him, and the sheep listen to his voice. He calls his own sheep by name and leads them out. When he has brought out all his own, he goes on ahead of them, and his sheep follow him because they know his voice. But they will never follow a stranger; in fact, they will run away from him because they do not recognize a stranger's voice." Jesus used this figure of speech, but they did not understand what he was telling them.

Therefore Jesus said again, "I tell you the truth, I am the gate for the sheep. All who ever came before me were thieves and robbers, but the sheep did not listen to them. I am the gate; whoever enters through me will be saved. He will come in and go out, and find pasture. The thief comes only to steal and kill and destroy; I have come that they may have life, and have it to the full.

Observations

This is a very familiar passage, perhaps too familiar. The first several dozen times it went past me in Sunday-school classes and sermons, I missed a key phrase or two. Jesus is assuming that the sheep (you and I) will listen to his voice (verse 3), so much so that we will come to know it (verse 4) and be able to separate its sound from that of a stranger. The notion of our taking the time to listen to God's voice was the foundational point of this chapter. Listening as a part of prayer is also requisite to developing a conversational relationship with God.

In this passage Jesus identifies himself as both the Good Shepherd and the gateway to abundant life. He is the friend, guardian, and companion of our soul. Learning to recognize the sound of his voice—and consequently being able to distinguish it from that of the thief and robber—is extremely important. In fact, it's a matter of life and death.

Reflection Questions

1. What does it mean to say that Jesus is the Shepherd of your soul?
2. What does it mean, in this passage, to say that Jesus is the "gate"?
3. What are your "rules of discernment"? How do you know if you are hearing from God or the thief and robber when you pray?
4. Have you ever heard God speak your name when listening for his voice?
5. What feelings did that cause to stir inside you?
6. What is the best way to understand what Jesus means by having "life…to the full"?
7. How would you describe the ways you experience companionship with God—and consequently learn to recognize his voice?

Meditation: Tuning Out the Static

Explanation

This chapter brings us to the end of our first section of the book. In it we have emphasized the theme of taking *time* for communication with God, and the meditation sections have focused on the purgation or letting go of the things that may prevent us from taking time for communion with God.

Meditation

Take a few minutes to practice becoming still and quiet before God. Then ask him to reveal the most powerful broadcasts or distractions that you hear instead of WGOD. Perhaps they are specific fears, attachments, or areas of emotional pain and wounding.

Once you feel one or more specific distractions have been communicated to you, audibly acknowledge them back to God as an agreement and confession. Then ask him to silence the volume of each distracting broadcast and increase the volume of thoughts he would like to share with you.

Spiritual Exercise: Tuning in WGOD

The Setup

Take a few minutes to take yourself through the Five Ps of Prayer. After you have become still and quiet before God, imagine that Jesus is sitting in front of you in an empty chair. Then ask him the following question: "What do you think of me?"

(*Note:* No need to allow more than a minute or two for his response. When you feel that God has communicated his answer, use the following checklist to help you evaluate the source of the communication.)

Indications of the Voice of God[5]

Channel 1 (WGOD)	Channel 2 (WSIN)

Nature of the Approach

leading and inviting	driving or pushing
quiet	loud
invited (wanted)	illegal entrance

Content

in line with scriptural principals	proof texts
has inner solution	outer solution
merciful	no mercy
corrects actual behavior	condemns broadly
convicts of sin (specific)	condemns worth
peacemaking	divisive

Relevance of the Content

now	future
practical and mundane	impractical and sensational
simple and definite	complicated and confused

Effects of the Content

love, peace, joy	anger, worry, discouragement
hope	hopelessness
faith increased	faith deflated
more understanding of others	despising of others

Hanging Out with God—All the Time

Frank Laubach

In the introduction to this book, I promised to end each section by introducing you to a person who fell head over heels in love with God and lived his or her life in constant conversation with him. I hope that their lives and their relationships with God inspire you to do the same and that they give you hope that you actually can experience the relationship with God that you long for.

The first of the three people I'd like you to know is Frank Laubach.

On March 23, 1930, Laubach wrote in his diary, "Can we have contact with God all the time? All the time awake, fall asleep in his arms, and awaken in His presence, can we attain that? Can we do His will all the time? Can we think His thoughts all the time?"[6]

When he posed these questions, forty-five-year-old Laubach was laboring under a cloud of profound dissatisfaction, despite his academic achievements—a B.A. from Princeton, a graduate degree from Union Theological Seminary, and an M.A. and Ph.D. in sociology from Columbia University—and his success as a missionary to the Philippines. For fifteen years he had won praise as a teacher, writer, and administrator.

Laubach's sterling achievements make it doubly puzzling when we read the self-assessment he made at the halftime of his life: "As for me, I never lived, I was half dead; I was a rotting tree."[7]

Even as his churches filled with converts, his heart was becoming crowded with loneliness, discouragement, and mild depression. Even after planting a seminary in the Philippines to train missionaries, he confessed that he had learned nothing of surrender and joy in Christ.

How can that be? Frank Laubach spoke of God daily. He had a devoted wife and family and all the trappings of success. Why was he so weighed down with doubt and despair?

Like Augustine, Laubach would forever feel restless and alone until nestled in the arms of God. He would forever feel lonely until awake to constant companionship with God.

Laubach determined to do something about his miserable condition and decided to make the rest of his life a continuous inner conversation with God in perfect responsiveness to God's will so that his own life could become rich with God's presence. All he could do was throw himself open to God. All he could do was raise the windows and unlock the doors of his soul. But he also knew that these simple acts of will were very important, and so he resolved to spend as many moments as possible listening and in determined sensitivity to God's presence.

In working his experiment, he invented something he called a "game with minutes." Laubach's game is a method of calling God to mind at least one second of each minute for the purpose of awareness and conversation.

As he began to live moment by moment in attentiveness to God's presence, Laubach experienced a remarkable change. By the end of the first month of the experiment, he had gained a sense of being carried along by God through the hours of cooperation with him in little things.

January 26

I am feeling God in each moment, by an act of will—willing that He shall direct these fingers that now strike this typewriter—willing that He shall pour through my steps as I walk, willing that He shall direct my words as I speak, and my very jaws as I eat![8]

March 1

The sense of being led by an unseen hand which takes mine while another hand reaches ahead and prepares the way, grows upon me daily.

I do not have to strain at all to find opportunity.... Perhaps a man who has been an ordained minister since 1914 ought to be ashamed to confess that he never before felt the joy of complete hourly, minute by minute—now what shall I call it?—more than surrender.[9]

April 18
God has caught me up with such sheer joy that I thought I never had known anything like it. God was so close and so amazingly lovely that I felt like melting all over with a strange and blissful contentment.... After an hour of close friendship with God my soul feels as clean as new-fallen snow.[10]

May 14
Now I *like* God's presence so much that when for a half hour or so He slips out of mind—as He does many times a day—I feel as though I had deserted Him, and as though I had lost something very precious in my life.[11]

June 3
The moment I turn to Him is like turning on an electric current which I feel through my whole being.[12]

September 21
For a lonesome man there is something infinitely homey and comforting in feeling God so close, so *everywhere!* Nowhere one turns is away from friendship, for God is smiling there.... It is difficult to convey to another the *joy* of having broken into the new sea of realizing God's "here-ness."[13]

When Laubach began his experiment, he was living among fierce Moros, an anti-Christian, Islamic tribe on Mindanao. Not long after he began to keep constant company with God, the Moros began to notice the difference. Two of the leading Muslim priests began telling people that Laubach could help them know God. And even though he never pretended to be anything other than a follower of Jesus, the Moros began to take Laubach into their hearts and lives, loving, trusting, and helping him without regard to their cultural and religious differences.[14]

Laubach's life began to flourish with the joy of God and even more amazing productivity. He birthed the "each one teach one" reading program that not only brought literacy to tens of thousands of the Moros tribe, but eventually to more than sixty million people around the world.

Laubach lived the second half of his life as God's constant companion. His life is a picture of the path of real change. He took the *time* to be with God, was *honest* about the condition of his heart, and trusted that God *desired* the same intimate relationship that he craved.

Part 2

Communion

It's Not
Just for Sunday Anymore

Chapter 5

Saying Yes to Fidelity

Turning Away from Other Loves

There is a spiritual longing that hovers around the edges of daily awareness, spiritual experiences and momentary recollections of the "home" that existed before self-definition and independent identity were established.

GERALD MAY

What God asks of us is a will which is no longer divided between him and any creature.... When we are in this disposition, all is well, and the most idle amusements turn to good works.

FRANÇOIS FENELON

My family has watched the movie *The Princess Bride* so many times we've memorized most of the dialogue, which can come in handy. Often after losing a tennis match, I catch myself semiquoting from the movie as I smile confidently at my opponent: "But I know a secret you do not know. I am not right-handed." Fortunately, most of the people who beat me in tennis know the scene I'm quoting and don't make me back up the claim.

As the movie opens, we see the heroine going about chores on a farm. Her name is Buttercup. (I know, but I still like the movie.) Soon we meet a young man who works on the farm and answers to the name Farm Boy.

Whenever Buttercup asks Farm Boy to do something for her, he always replies, "As you wish." And that's all he ever says to her.

As they grow into their hormones, Buttercup seems to be developing a crush on Farm Boy. One day as he is about to leave the room, she asks him to fetch her a pitcher, which is within easy reach for her. Farm Boy walks over, then stares into her eyes, lifts the pitcher, and in a breathy whisper says, "As you wish."

In that moment, returning his gaze, Buttercup realizes that every time he has said, "As you wish," he was really saying, "I love you."

And when we respond to God with the words, "As you wish," we are doing the same.

With this chapter our focus shifts from *conversation with God* to the deeper notion of *communion*—intimate sharing, fellowship, and rapport. As with any romantic relationship, conversation is not the end goal but merely the gateway to deeper levels of intimacy. At the heart of communion with God is the whisper, "As you wish." In communion, two hearts begin to beat as one and, at least for brief moments, reflect a single will.

WILLINGNESS VERSUS WILLFULNESS

Scripture repeatedly draws a distinction between willfulness and willingness. Even prior to the first stain of ink on papyrus to form the words, "In the beginning," Satan had already fallen from grace because he chose willfulness. He attempted to seize power, to be as God instead of continuing to surrender to the will of his Creator. Father Adam and Mother Eve had to make a similar choice between eating from the Tree of Life and eating from the Tree of the Knowledge of Good and Evil.

I believe the Tree of Life represents a willingness to stay in fellowship with God, connected like branches in a vine, whereas the Tree of the Knowledge of Good and Evil symbolizes a continuation of the willful choice Satan made to be as God. The two trees represent the most fundamental choice a spiritual being can make: the choice between willfulness and willingness. Let's take a closer look at each of these choices.

God told Adam and Eve not to eat—consume, make a part of themselves—the Tree of the Knowledge of Good and Evil. Why? What's so wrong with knowing the difference between good and evil?

According to Ted Dorman,[1] in the Old Testament "the knowledge of good and evil" refers to moral autonomy, or the ability to make moral choices without being accountable to anyone else. Initially, small children must depend on their parents to guide them in making moral choices, but as they grow, they should develop an understanding of the knowledge of good and evil for themselves,[2] since their parents will not always be around. For human relationships, this type of knowledge is desirable.

But the Genesis account does not describe a human parent-child relationship. Adam and Eve's "parent" was the Creator of the universe. To desire moral autonomy in relationship to God is to desire to be like God, to be God. Adam and Eve's disobedience was a matter of unbelief. Their distrust that God had their best interests at heart resulted in a movement away from living connected to God.

One of the greatest insults one person can give to another is to say, "I don't trust you." Imagine those words in the mouth of your spouse, child, or parent. This is exactly what Adam and Eve said to God. "I don't trust you to know what is best for me; I must become independent and take matters into my own hands." The original sin was a fear-driven incapacity to trust and resulted in the loss of the willingness to live in a submissive relationship to the alluring mystery and community that is God.

Conversely, the Tree of Life, I believe, symbolizes the willingness to live life connected to God. If you will permit me some license with the symbolism here, I see the River of Life as the very person and presence of God. The River of Life flowed near and watered the Tree of Life and became present in its fruit.

Eating from the Tree of Life is to choose willingness, to choose to stay connected to God, keeping God *in* us. His presence waters our soul and causes the
fruit of his Spirit to become the character of our life. The Lord's Supper con-
sists of fruit from the Tree of Life—the real and indwelling presence of Christ.

Over and over again and throughout Scripture, we see people faced with
the same choice between willfulness and willingness, and we see God's punishment for willfulness and faithful reward for willingness. For instance:

- Cain made a willful choice to ignore God's requirement for a blood
  sacrifice and then to kill his brother, Abel. Cain's choice caused him to
  fall even further than his parents into the pit of despair.
- As apple juice dripped from their lips, the willful builders of Babel sang,
  "Come, let us build ourselves a city, with a tower that reaches to the
  heavens, so that we may make a name for ourselves and not be scattered
  over the face of the whole earth" (Genesis 11:4). Their desire to be separate from and equal with God resulted in divisions among themselves.
- Abraham became the father of a great nation in the exact moment he
  stood over his own son, knife drawn, and became willing to say to
  God, "Your will and not mine be done." Through this act of willingness Abram demonstrated radical trust in God, saying, "As you wish,"
  even as every fiber in his body shouted, "No!"
- Although he took a forty-year sabbatical from the crime scene of his
  willful murder of an Egyptian, Moses eventually threw down his rod
  (the symbol of his ability to protect himself) in the very presence of an
  enemy, Pharaoh, and came to realize that his self-sufficiency had been a
  snake all along.
- God extended the Israelites' six-month trip across the wilderness for forty
  years because they chose willfulness at almost every fork in the road.
- David followed the path of willingness to confront Goliath, but he
  took the willful shortcut to Bathsheba's place.

- A young Jewish girl, after being told by an angel that she would conceive a baby as a virgin, said, "I am the Lord's servant.… May it be to me as you have said" (Luke 1:38). Willingness made Mary God's first communion chalice.

Willingness means learning to embrace a state of continuous surrender to the will of God. The gateway to deeper levels of communion with God, willingness is foundational to the Christian journey. In willingness we surrender our separateness from God and resolve to continue on the road that ultimately leads home. Willingness enables us to splash freely in the river of God's sufficiency on a day-by-day, hour-by-hour, moment-by-moment basis. Willingness means saying yes to God over the loud protests of body and ego.

Willfulness, by contrast, sets us apart from God, the fundamental essence of life, by attempting to master, direct, control, or otherwise manipulate our existence. Willfulness says, "I want to be God." It leads away from relationship and to the hell of isolation from the loving community of being, meaning, and love, and from community with the Father, Son, and Holy Spirit.

Willingness says, "Whoopee!" to the mystery of being alive in Christ in each moment. In choosing willingness, we let go of grasping and come out of hiding. Willfulness says either "No" or "Yes, but…"

The church has prized, devotional literature, which begins with a declaration of willingness. For example, "The LORD is my shepherd" and "Our Father in heaven…your will be done." The most accepted creed of the Christian faith—about the only one upon which all Christian bodies can agree—is, "Jesus is Lord."

But those who join this club pay staggering dues. Members must make a profession of the willing statements: "Jesus is the Lord of my life—I am not" and "Your kingdom come, and my kingdom go."

Most people will not surrender the reigns of their life to God apart from a crisis of some sort. That's what it took for me.

A MOMENT OF HONESTY

Not long ago I was sitting with two close friends and enjoying lunch. Since one is a priest, it wasn't long before he asked, "What are each of you doing to keep your soul healthy?"

I blurted out, "I keep screwing up."

I looked up and saw two concerned faces, each wearing question marks. Neither knew until that moment that I had been going through a tough period. I told them that I was in the middle of a gloomy time, and I knew very well what had caused the lights to dim. For several months I had been taking the willful fork in the road, each time moving further from conversation and communion with God. At work, at home, and in all my closest relationships, I had slipped back into old patterns of self-absorption and had become more demanding that I get my own way. In my shame, I had been avoiding any awareness of God's loving presence.

For a long period of time, years before, God had showered me with grace. I think he knew I needed that in order to be freed from a legalistic background. For more than a decade, his words of love and forgiveness echoed in my ears as his portrait changed in my mind from that of a cosmic sheriff to the prodigal's father.

But I had left the cork out of the bottle, and the expensive taste of radical grace had begun to spoil. I had allowed it to become cheap and myself complacent. It had become too easy to live by the motto, "I'll do what I want and ask for forgiveness later."

So as mercy eventually demands, justice stepped out of the shadows. God had begun to allow me to experience some of the natural and logical consequences of willfulness—the isolation and despair produced by selfish choices, the crushing weight of trying to be God. These consequences had become very painful, and I was beginning to feel more and more alone.

But I also knew that the pain was my friend. Like an abscessed tooth, or flesh searing over a flame, it was telling me something was wrong. The pain had intensified so much that it motivated me to do something sensible. Stop. Turn around. Face God. Drop to my knees. Ask for forgiveness.

Within a few days, pain would, once again, cause me to back up and take the right road, to eat again from the Tree of Life. Without the pain, I would've been as happy as a pig in slop. So in all honesty, the best thing I had done for my spiritual growth was to screw up. Grief as a natural consequence of willfulness can push you to your knees and light up the path of willingness. It can make you look at God and whisper again, "As you wish."

How Joey Got His Dad to Stop Drinking

I'd like to tell you the story of someone else who became willing to change course and head back home to willingness. I met him a few months ago.

The gathering was in a back room of an Olive Garden restaurant. I arrived and took the last seat. About twenty others were sitting around tables that formed a hollow square. I was about half-finished with my pasta when a silver-haired gentleman began to call the meeting to order by tapping his glass with a spoon.

"Hello," he said. "My name is Bill, and I'm an alcoholic."

"Hello, Bill," the crowd responded.

Bill had a special announcement to make. One of the regulars had lost a son. George's boy, Joey, had passed away earlier that week. The way the announcement was made let me know I was probably the only one present who didn't already know. As it turned out, most had attended the funeral.

George wanted to address the group. He stood up and seemed at ease in front of people. A smile was on his face, but his eyes were red and puffy. He said something I'll never forget. With his voice breaking, he said, "I just want to thank God in front of all you friends that he saw fit to bless me with a mentally retarded son."

Heads began to nod as he continued. "Joey taught me the most important lessons in life. Because of Joey, I became a much wiser man."

He wasn't able to get many more words out. He started crying really hard, and then two women got up and gave him bear hugs.

George sat down, and Bill stood up. He said a few nice things about Joey and asked if anyone had something to say to George. Everyone in the room did. Each began by giving his or her name and saying "I'm an alcoholic" and concluded with a warm story about how Joey had touched his or her life. Joey was an angel unaware.

When the meeting ended, I was in no hurry to get back to work. To my surprise George came over and shook my hand before leaving. "I guess this all sounded pretty strange to you. But if you've got a second I'd like to tell you the rest of the story."

I immediately sat down. So did George.

"When Joey came into this world nineteen years ago, he was born with a problem," he began. "It wasn't his brain. It was worse than that. He had an alcoholic for a father.

"We could tell Joey wasn't going to be like most other babies. He was born special. The doctor told us the next day he probably wouldn't ever get any smarter than a five- or six-year-old.

"But like I said, that was the least of his problems. He had a drunk for a father. Right then and there I knew what I had to do. I decided I had to change what could be changed. It took a year, finding God, and a group like this, but we did it. God, these friends, and I.

"For my Joey's first birthday, he got a brand-new daddy for a present. He never suspected that it was he who did the giving. But he wasn't done yet.

"Years passed. I came to realize that I had fallen in love with my own healthy brain. I loved to show it off—display for people how smart I was. I loved to use my wit and reason to get compliments, win acceptance, and sell cars. But Joey could care less. My boy would never be able to appreciate my brain. He'd never look up to me because of my cleverness.

"At first I got depressed about that and angry. One of the most important people in my life would never look at what I could accomplish and say, 'Way to go!'

"I wondered how I could ever impress him with how smart I was. I had a few words with God about my predicament that weren't very bright.

"It wasn't long before I began to see there *was* a way to impress the boy. I noticed he got excited every time I took the time to just be *with* him. It only took my being there to get his hands waving and his face beaming. That's all he wanted."

"I think I see," I said.

"That was some present Joey gave me, wasn't it? He let me know I was enough. Me. My being with him was enough to make him happy. Me, just as I am, was enough to put a smile on that little face. Performance and cleverness weren't necessary for Joey to love me. He just wanted us to be together."

At that point George's voice started breaking up again. He excused himself and gave me a quick pat on the back and went to gather up his papers. I sat there as George collected his things into an old, brown brief case. Joey had passed on another great gift, through his father; I wanted to unwrap it carefully before I stood up.

George surrendered the reins of his life to God because he realized how much Joey would need him. What started as a painful crisis became the motivation for George to begin walking the path of willing surrender.

But that was just Part A. Joey also taught his dad to be a part of a relationship founded on unconditional love. Joey's boundless love helped to heal George. George quit drinking because of the shock of Joey as a son, but Joey's love took away the desire to drink. George no longer needed alcohol to provide brief vacations from his emotional pain—willingness and love healed most of it at the source.

Joey's love for everybody and George's love for Joey had healed the pain this father had been trying to drown. The support and accountability provided by his AA group sealed the deal, helping George to stay on the path of willingness. Yes, love is the only healthy cure for emotional anguish. And willingness is the only road that heads out of hell.

"You know," I told George. "Jesus was too special to fit in with this world too. And just like your boy, he helped a lot of people before leaving early."

WHY ALL THIS AA TALK

I had attended that meeting as a voyeur. Having referred dozens of people to AA, I wanted to see what went on behind closed doors. I don't tell you this out of defensiveness. I wrestle with a much more deadly addiction than alcoholism. I'm addicted to willfulness, being in control, making the decisions on my own, being right—in short, being God. It's the main way I screw up. It's the reason I continue to battle the urges to grasp and hide.

I've been just like George—headed down the wrong road and away from communion and community. And for anyone who has made willful choices, there is only one way out: admitting that our life, which we've lived on our own terms, is broken, and only God can fix it.

At that point of humble transparency it becomes possible to turn around and begin jogging down the road less traveled, a much narrower path crowded with lepers and prostitutes. It leads away from the illusion of self-sufficiency and into God's outstretched arms.

In some ways desperate addicts find it easier to embrace willingness. But for the mercy of pain, a complacent Sunday-school teacher may balk at the notion of needing a designated driver for his or her life. But we are all—from addicts to apostles—just like our original parents, Adam and Eve. The craving to be God is still much stronger than the attraction to be a willing servant.

Deep communion with God begins with raw honesty, followed by the radical surrender of all illusions of power and control. Such honesty fosters real intimacy, sharing, and change. Blessed are we when we have screwed up so badly that we've become willing to try anything. Blessed are we when life's responsibilities close all doors but one. Desperation can become the doorway to restored communion with God.

Dallas Willard, in *Renovation of the Heart,* goes so far as to claim that "any successful plan for spiritual formation, whether for individuals or groups, will in fact be significantly similar to the Alcoholics Anonymous program."[3]

And in case anyone should miss the irony of unlikely ragamuffins once again leading the parade into the kingdom, he observes, "The AA program originated and gained its power from Christian sources, to meet the needs that Christian institutions at the same time should have been meeting *but were not.*"[4]

Be wary of any spiritual path that does not demand a total surrender to the will of God while offering both community and accountability. When we admit that life apart from willing surrender is a broken toy that we cannot fix on our own, we take a giant leap into the arms of God, into communion. When we see our addictions—be they alcohol, pornography, control, workaholism, or whatever—as rival lovers, we can look at God through tear-filled eyes and say, "As you wish."

Jesus knew willingness was foundational to authentic Christian living and necessary for staying connected to God. That's why he made it the major theme of his commencement address to his disciples.

FROM TRAGEDY TO TRIUMPH

What would you do if you knew you only had twenty-four hours of freedom before being arrested and put to death?

That's the question Jesus wrestled with on the Thursday of Passion Week as he gathers his closest friends for a final meal together. He gets up from the table, takes off his outer clothing, and begins to wash their dirty feet—even the two attached to Judas. The King of kings does a job that is beneath the dignity of a slave, and his doing so takes self-emptying to a new low and raises love to new heights. His friends don't understand, but they will.

With the water of his love still dripping from his hands, Jesus helps prepare his friends by telling them what is about to happen. And he continues to comfort them with talk of his love for them and the promise of a holy Helper.

Then, he lets them in on the most important mystery in the universe. Even Paul doesn't figure this one out until Colossians 1:26-27—the great mystery revealed is *Christ in you,* the hope of glory. We can live connected to Jesus and the Father just as branches are *in* a vine. We can be *in* Christ, and Christ can be in us, just as he and the Father are connected: one.

Perhaps the disciples don't understand, and this lesson is so important. So Jesus gives them an object lesson, saying, "Just as bread and wine can be taken in and become present to each cell in a body, I can be taken in to energize each atom of you."

At the end of all the comforting words and object lessons, Jesus wraps up his five-chapter commencement address about staying connected to God with a prayer of intercession for himself (John 17:1-5), his friends (John 17:6-19), and for you and me (John 17:20-26).

Then he leaves with three of his closest friends and goes to the Garden of Gethsemane. Maybe he wanted them—and all humankind—to see that what first went wrong in a garden would be set right in one. He sweats drops of blood, his humanity so desperately wanting to go the safer route of willfulness. Three times he cries out to his Father, "If you are willing, take this cup from me." Three times he adds to and amplifies the words of Abraham and Mary, his mother: "Yet not my will, but yours be done."

The last thing Jesus did before his arrest is to go to a garden for a conversation with his Father. Like the first Adam, he encounters two trees in the garden. Unlike the first Adam, he eats only from the Tree of Life and chooses willing surrender to the will of God. A garden tragedy becomes a garden triumph.

Jesus' acceptance of the cross is the ultimate symbol of willingness—obedience, even unto death. His sacred heart hung at the point of intersection between the vertical (the will of God) and the horizontal (the will of man). On the cross, Jesus told his Father, "As you wish." He knew it was the best way to say, "I love you."

Bible Study: The Two Trees

Text: Genesis 2:8-9,15-17; 3:4-10

Now the LORD God had planted a garden in the east, in Eden; and there he put the man he had formed. And the LORD God made all kinds of trees grow out of the ground—trees that were pleasing to the eye and good for food. In the middle of the garden were the tree of life and the tree of the knowledge of good and evil....

The LORD God took the man and put him in the Garden of Eden to work it and take care of it. And the LORD God commanded the man, "You are free to eat from any tree in the garden; but you must not eat from the tree of the knowledge of good and evil, for when you eat of it you will surely die."...

"You will not surely die," the serpent said to the woman. "For God knows that when you eat of it your eyes will be opened, and you will be like God, knowing good and evil."

When the woman saw that the fruit of the tree was good for food and pleasing to the eye, and also desirable for gaining wisdom, she took some and ate it. She also gave some to her husband, who was with her, and he ate it. Then the eyes of both of them were opened, and they realized they were naked; so they sewed fig leaves together and made coverings for themselves.

Then the man and his wife heard the sound of the LORD God as he was walking in the garden in the cool of the day, and they hid from the LORD God among the trees of the garden. But the LORD God called to the man, "Where are you?"

He answered, "I heard you in the garden, and I was afraid because I was naked; so I hid."

Observations

You've probably heard the story about the man who loses his footing while inspecting the gaping beauty of the Grand Canyon. The ground begins to erode under his feet, and he slides over the edge of a steep cliff. Grabbing wildly for life, he latches on to a scraggly bush growing from the side of the canyon wall. With his feet dangling in midair and his fingers entwined with thin, leafy limbs, he cries out, "God, please help me!"

Immediately, a voice deeper than James Earl Jones's resonates from below. "I'm here for you, Son. Let go. I've got you."

A few seconds pass in silence as beads of sweat begin to emerge on the man's forehead. Then he cries out again, "Anyone got a better idea?"

Sometimes the choice of willingness seems just that scary and the consequences as large as life. The preceding passages are about more than the choice of eating apples or oranges. They describe the drama we awake to each morning. Will we choose trust, surrender, and connection to the will of God, or will we continue to live on our own terms? Ultimately, it's a life-or-death decision.

Reflection Questions

1. What are some practical ways in which you can eat from the Tree of Life on a daily basis?

2. Describe a time in which you ate from the Tree of the Knowledge of Good and Evil, when you exercised autonomy from God.

3. Adam and Eve's lack of trust that God had their best interests at heart caused them first to grasp (take control and try to be God) and then to hide (move away from God's presence because of shame). Have you ever hidden from awareness of God's presence because of a feeling of shame? If yes, what happened that gave you the courage to come out of hiding (advice from a friend, reading a special passage of Scripture, or a whisper from God)?

4. How does willingness and willfulness relate to the story of the Fall?

5. What does it mean to say that Jesus went into a garden to make right what first went wrong in a garden?

Meditation: Twelve Steps Toward Home

Explanation
What follows are the twelve steps of the AA model presented as a prayer. Please take a few moments to pray the steps.

Meditation[5]

1. Lord, apart from you, my life becomes broken, and I don't know how to fix it. Please help me. Do for me what I cannot do for myself.

2. Father, I believe that your Son, Jesus, can restore my soul. Jesus, please be the Physician I need. I invite you to enter my heart and bring healing to any disease you find there. Only you can make me whole. Dissolve all that keeps me separate from you.

3. My will is yours, Jesus. Although my fingers are probably crossed right now, I do want you to make any changes in my life that are needed (especially in my thought life—and the way I imagine you) until I no longer want to be in control of my life. As you prayed in the garden, "Your will and not mine be done."

4. While it seems more than I can stomach, whisper to me about the times and places where I caused pain to those you love—those I should have loved more.

5. I confess to you now, Jesus, my sinful patterns of thoughts, emotions, behaviors, and interactions with others that have resulted in so much pain and suffering.

6./7. Jesus, I am ready to become whole and, by your presence, holy. Forgive my sins, I beg. Be a powerful presence in the deepest parts of me. Teach me to cooperate with you until I have taken on your mind. Let my character be your own.

8./9. Reveal to me, Jesus, the names of all the people I have harmed and also how you would like for me to pursue reconciliation with them.

10. Lord, remind me each night to sit with you and ask myself how the day has gone. If I have slipped back into old patterns of behavior that are harmful to myself and others, reveal it to me and show me what I should do. I want to keep a short account, Father. Please help me to do so.

11. Help me to put activities in my life each day that enable me to better sense your presence. I want to enjoy time with you and conversations that become deep and intimate. Fill my day with little reminders that you enjoy this too.

12. Thank you, God, for healing my soul and inviting me to participate in your community of love. Use me to help others enjoy what we enjoy together now.

Spiritual Exercise: Centering Prayer

Brief Background

Much has been written about "centering prayer," a form of contemplative communion with God that is based on the fourteenth-century English classic *The Cloud of Unknowing*. Fathers Basil Pennington and Thomas Keating, both Trappist monks, are perhaps the leading proponents of this manner of being with God.

Exercise in Centering Prayer: Guidelines

1. *Sit relaxed and quiet.* Take a few moments to review the Five Ps of Prayer and use them to become relaxed and quiet in God's presence.
2. *Be with God in faith and love.* Enjoy the awareness that God is everywhere, including the center of your being. In love, surrender all of yourself to him, your whole attention and all of who you are. You may even wish to say to God: *I am all yours, Lord. Do with me whatever you will.*
3. *Focus on a simple word.* Take up a word that reflects your love for God. Perhaps it will be your favorite name for the Lord: Jesus, Lord, Friend, Abba. Quietly and gently say the word, and let it repeat itself as you remain with God, open to him, letting him be present to you any way he wants.
4. *Gently return to being with the Lord.* Whenever you become aware of anything else, simply, gently return to the Lord with the use of your prayer word as a point of focus.
5. *Allow a closing prayer to pray within.* For a period of approximately twenty minutes, simply be with God in a posture of trust and willingness.

At the end of your prayer time, let a prayer such as the Lord's Prayer (the Our Father) pray itself within you.

Chapter 6

Fear of Total Commitment

How Communion Exposes My False Self

You were taught, with regard to your former way of life, to put off your old self, which is being corrupted by its deceitful desires; to be made new in the attitude of your minds; and to put on the new self, created to be like God in true righteousness and holiness.

EPHESIANS 4:22-24

For God hath not given us the spirit of fear; but of power, and of love, and of a sound mind.

2 TIMOTHY 1:7, KJV

No account of Christian spirituality is complete if it fails to give a central place to love. God is love. He has poured this love into our hearts through the Holy Spirit (Romans 5:5). Offering us his love, he desires that we become like him—great lovers.

DAVID G. BENNER

When we open our heart to God's presence with a sincere "As you wish," our true self—or as the apostle Paul would say, our "new self"—awakens and becomes vibrant. Such times produce what Gray Temple calls a "molten soul."[1] Our hearts bubble with the life of God, warmed by the embrace of our Father.

We treasure such encounters with God because they let us know beyond doubt that God is real and deeply in love with us. They confirm a long-held intuition that the truest part of us is most alive when abandoned to God.

For days after such a meeting we continue to see the world differently. Our feet hardly touch the ground when we walk. Relationship difficulties dissolve in the heat of love. Money, fame, and power seem insignificant. During these molten times we want only to live continually in that melted moment.

But then our soul begins to congeal, and other sensations step to center stage. Perhaps we first notice that the magic is gone while we're sitting in church. We're too hot. The pew's fabric irritates our back. A baby cries, and we're annoyed that his young parents didn't make use of the nursery. We begin to think about the bills we need to pay as the worship music fades to background noise. When the pastor makes an announcement, we realize we have not talked to him in several months and wonder if he still holds us in high esteem. Then we tune out our surroundings and begin to write a to-do list for tomorrow. Suddenly, we realize we're mouthing the words to the chorus, "He Is Lord." Amazed that the congregation is still singing, we wonder, *Have mercy—how long will the music go on?*

Mere days after an encounter with God that resurrects our true self, our false self assumes its familiar place behind the control panel of our life. No more romance. The roller-coaster ride of our soul goes from lukewarm to white-hot to cold. What's going on here? Why do we let our false self dethrone our true self?

Our predicament reminds me of this story about a dog and a rabbit. A man looks out his window and sees a horrible sight. His dog has his neighbor's prized pet, a black-and-white rabbit, in its mouth and is shaking it like a rag doll. The man bolts from his house and shouts at his dog until it drops the rabbit. As he gazes down at the motionless form, his worst fears are confirmed. The rabbit is dead.

The man scoops up the bunny and takes it into his house. He puts it in the sink and washes away the dirt and grime. And then he blows its fur dry with his hair dryer.

Noticing that his neighbors are still away, he takes the rabbit and sneaks into their backyard. Carefully he places the expired pet back in the metal cage where it has lived for years. He props it up with a stick, lays a carrot at its feet, and returns home.

great stuff!

A few hours later he is startled by screams. Assuming the dead bunny has been discovered, he runs outside to comfort his neighbor. But it's worse than he thinks.

"What's wrong?" he asks with false ignorance.

"It's my rabbit!" his neighbor shrieks hysterically. "Buggs died last week, and we buried him in the backyard. And now he's sitting up in his cage, eating a carrot!"[2]

Why do we dig up the stinking carcass of our false self and prop it back in its former place? To answer that question, let's explore how the false self usurps the throne and what seduces us to let it stay there.

How the True Self Gets Dethroned

At the root and center of our being is what Scripture calls the "image and likeness of God," the *imago dei*. At the center of who we are is the desire to be reunited with God and live as his reflection and representative. Our true self is very much like God; our true self is love. For us to come home to love is like a drop of water finding the ocean.

When we become molten, we experience the delight of willing surrender and the awareness of an awakened true self. This initial stage of communion with God feels great, but later stages hurt like the devil.

As we learned in chapter 3, fear, the original sin, has been injected into human consciousness like snake venom, poisoning us with the belief that Father doesn't know best. I do. I am the center and the only being in the universe who can be trusted.

In a stupor, we begin clutching for golden apples and hide in shame behind barriers that block the light of God's presence. Then we pack our bags and move away from the garden of God's will to the tiny island of ego, where we can reign as monarchs. Rulers, yes, but all the while hearing two voices. One invites us back to sanity. "Take off the tin crown," it says. "Leave the island and come back home."

The other voice just keeps saying, "You are the only one you can trust to be in control of your life. Only you know what's best for you. Better look out for number one."

This tug of war between the true and false self always comes into clear focus after a person makes a serious commitment to willingness. A prolonged state of willing surrender always exposes the controlling nature of the false self. Willingness brings out into the light our deepest fears and our most cherished idols, those God-substitutes we use to mollify our fears.

For centuries the devotion masters have described this ongoing tension between the true self—love and its desire to return to a life of intimacy and surrender—and the false self—a fear-driven identity of separation and autonomy. The self that I am called to be from the dawn of eternity is the self that I am *in* Christ. It is my eternal self, my real identity, the part of me that desires nothing more than a relationship of continual conversation, communion, and union with God.

But my false self resists Christ's invitation to reign *in* me. It wants to be the ruler, even if for a tiny kingdom and for a wisp of time. At the core of my false ways of being is what Thomas Merton called a sinful refusal to surrender to God's will.

If a false sense of "I" sits on the throne of our hearts, we will not enjoy life in the kingdom. This false self, the usurper, wants to maintain control at all costs and fears having the real self return to the throne to rule with wisdom. The false self does not want us to develop a conversational and communal relationship with God that has us whispering, "As *you* wish." Willingness kills the false self.

Conversely, the true self can only rule from a position of close communion with God, drawing on divine wisdom and maintaining an intimate fellowship with the true King. Unless we live in a state of connection to God, even the wisest of us is no match for the great deceiver of souls.

We become vulnerable to such fraud to the extent that we have come to believe that God offers his love on a conditional basis and is ultimately weak or unwise, and consequently, we take our well-being into our own hands. The true self gets dethroned when we fear that God can't be trusted, and so we seek wisdom from sources other than him.

VULNERABLE TO THE IDOLS OF PLEASURE, ESTEEM, AND SECURITY

As was pointed out earlier, our refusal to continue in willing surrender leaves us separate and vulnerable. Continuing to live outside the garden leaves us at the mercy of the same demon that caused the muddle—fear. Fear whispers that we need more than independence; we also need idols, God-substitutes. So we look for solace in *pleasure* (how I can be gratified), *esteem* (what others think of me), and *security* (what I have and what I do).

Without God as an ally, our false self becomes very dependent on these idols, and so we fill our palace with statues of false gods. As we latch onto these idols—career, success, money, positions of influence, control, alcohol, and prescription and nonprescription drugs—they become behavioral and emotional narcotics we use to treat our fears and allay our anxieties. To a measure, these "drugs" work, but even as they bring some amount of relief, we become increasingly addicted to them, and our grasping grows even stronger.

A Parable of the True and False Self

This is a retelling of a retelling of a Jewish folk legend about King Solomon from *Money and the Meaning of Life* by Jacob Needleman.[3]

Solomon is to build a temple, a place for communion with God. He discovers, however, that he needs a special tool, a *shamir*, for cutting the heavy stones. To his dismay he learns that Asmodeus, chief of demons, possesses the instrument.

Solomon quickly devises a plan to take the tool from Asmodeus. He sends his most trusted servant to the mountain of darkness, the home of Asmodeus, to trick him into surrendering the *shamir*.

While Asmodeus is away, Solomon's servant pours wine into the well. Asmodeus returns, drinks buckets from the well, and falls into a stupor.

The servant, armed with chains and Solomon's signet ring, captures the demon and brings him back to Solomon's palace.

Through dialogue with Asmodeus, Solomon learns the whereabouts of the special cutting tool and has it retrieved. He also learns that not only will the *shamir* cut through stone, it also symbolizes the penetrating force of God that can cut through a hardened heart and allow life to flourish where none had been before.

Solomon uses the *shamir* to complete the temple.

Long afterward, with Asmodeus still in chains, Solomon goes to him. "Tell me," says the king to Asmodeus, "what is

(continued)

the nature of your power? How is it that you ruled so mightily over humans?"

Asmodeus recognizes his opportunity for freedom and devises a plan to trick Solomon. "I'll tell you the secret, but first you must unbind me and let me hold your ring." He knew the ring symbolized Solomon's true identity.

Solomon agrees to the demon's terms, unbinds Asmodeus, and hands him the sacred ring for inspection. In a lightning flash, Asmodeus grows to enormous size. Quick as a snake strike, Asmodeus swallows Solomon and then spews him with such force that he lands in a distant country, far away from Jerusalem, the city of God, and far away from the temple, the presence of God.

Asmodeus throws the signet ring into the ocean and shakes the earth with his laughter. He enters the inner chambers of the palace, puts on royal garments and the king's crown, and changes his face to look like that of Solomon. Then the demon king sits on the throne in place of the real king.

Asmodeus had answered Solomon's question. His power lay in his ability to take on the appearance of the rightful ruler, to appear to be the true self within! The power of all the other demons derives from this chief power of Asmodeus. And the chief weakness of man is his vulnerability to a false sense of "I" sitting on the throne of the human heart.

Mercifully, the legend continues.

Solomon tries to make a new life for himself. Clothed in the rags of his former glory, he lives the life of the poorest beggar. He wanders the countryside crying out, "I am Solomon! I was king of Jerusalem!" He becomes a target for insults and stones. Brought low in every respect, he experiences his nothingness apart from his true identity.

Meanwhile, Asmodeus rules in Solomon's place and commits many atrocities and excesses. Slowly, Solomon's splendid kingdom is devastated. The temple becomes as silent as a tomb.

With time, things improve for Solomon. He falls in love with a woman who, incredibly, returns his love. Together they build a modest life.

Then one day, while fishing, Solomon catches a large fish. Beaming with pride, he brings it home for his wife to see. But when he cuts it open for cleaning, his signet rings falls to the ground.

Solomon picks it up and with trembling hands places it on his finger. Immediately he stands tall and radiates his former majesty. Though dressed as a beggar, he is King Solomon. He is again his true self.

His wife recognizes the miracle and insists that he make the journey back to Jerusalem to assume his throne. And he does with her at his side.

In the last scene of the legend, King Solomon, still wearing rags, walks into the palace and confronts Asmodeus. The true king meets eye to eye with the false king. Slowly, Solomon raises his dirty hand and shows Asmodeus the sacred ring. Asmodeus vanishes in an instant, vacating the throne. Prosperity returns to the kingdom. The nightmare is over.

In fact, too often our lives look like scenes from the musical *Little Shop of Horrors*.

The *Little Shop of Horrors* is a dark, musical comedy about Seymour Krelborn, a downtrodden geek working in Mushnik's flower shop on Skid Row. As the film opens, things are not going well for the flower business, Seymour, or his romantic aspirations. Seymour pines for Audrey, a shrill-voiced flower arranger who also works in Mushnik's. Audrey is currently involved with a sadistic, motorcycle-riding, laughing-gas addict. But soon things change for Seymour. He discovers a small Venus's-flytrap and brings the strange looking plant back to the flower shop and sets it in the window. Immediately the exotic plant begins to attract patrons who come in to ogle it but then stay to buy flowers.

Seymour doesn't know that the flytrap, which he names Audrey II, is really a monstrous plant from outer space that needs human blood to survive. Driven by his desire to keep the shop afloat (he doesn't want to lose the opportunity to see Audrey I every day), Seymour begins to feed the plant drops of his own blood.

But it quickly becomes obvious that Seymour's lifeblood is not enough. The plant's appetite grows, and then people begin to disappear. When Audrey II's lips seek Audrey I and a marketing agent presents the opportunity of having a plant like Audrey II in every home on the planet, Seymour realizes the horror of the plant's intention, and the stage is set for a climactic showdown between Seymour and the blood-sucking pod.

This musical vividly illustrates the two things that fear can do in our lives. Much of the time it drives us to seek after idols that dull our pain and allow our false self to continue its reign. Initially, this is where fear leads Seymour. Audrey II is the quintessential picture of an idol. At first the plant seems so small and harmless, even cute and desirable. As it works its magic, Seymour's fortunes improve. He stays empowered and in control, but, oh, the price is high. It costs Seymour his very lifeblood, and his kingdom becomes a dark wasteland.

But there is good news in all this bad news. Fear can also motivate us to give up living in the dark and run back to connection with God, the source of love that can flush out fear. In the musical, love gives Seymour the power to destroy the idol that has dulled his sense of truth. In love he finds both his strength and his truest self. In the end our discomfort and fear can draw us to God and keep our souls molten and alive so that love can continue to draw us toward union.

A Day of Reckoning

A few years back I came face to face with my own Audrey II. I was completing a thirty-day retreat in Ignatian spirituality. The setting was a large retreat center on the bank of a bright blue lake in upstate New York.

As part of one of the prayer exercises, I was contemplating the end of my life. The only instruction I was given was to picture myself on my deathbed and let my imagination take it from there.

What I saw was shocking and life-changing. I pictured myself lying on a metal-frame hospital bed in a stark white room. I saw the bed, a column of equipment for monitoring my vital functions, a sideways column of light from an open window, a dutiful nurse, and a door. That's all. I looked around for my wife and children, but they were nowhere to be found. I looked for friends. None. As I continued to scan the room for a sign of grief or compassion, I saw two file cabinets in the corner of the room.

I asked the nurse what was in the cabinets. She looked sad as she pulled open each drawer. The cabinets were crammed full of all the papers, columns, articles, and books I had written. I started to cry.

Alone on my deathbed, I realized that my false self had won. It had continued to deceive me with the notion that I was of limited value to anyone unless I produced and earned. It had kept my true identity as God's beloved child a secret from me.

My writing projects had become life-sucking idols in my life. They had started small, but I had not been able to resist what they had to offer: an illusion of success, meaning, and purpose, the chance for new job opportunities, and more money. In the end I could see that these idols had grown and consumed my true self and the time that others needed from me.

This exercise proved to be transforming. Or to put it more succinctly, it scared the hell out of me. From that day forward I have attempted to spend regular times of solitude each day, week, and month for the purpose of listening to God tell me about my true identity, how secure I am in him, and how much I am loved. When I can muster the courage, I ask him to be honest with me about which of my two selves is sitting on the throne. I have also attempted to make every career decision based more on the quality of life and time away from the office it affords me rather than on esteem and recognition.

Now don't get me wrong. By now I hope you have seen that this journey we are on is not linear. We can move in and out of conversation, communion, and union. So I'm not always home by five, I still say yes to too many projects, and I frequently find myself being envious of colleagues who have a more bulky résumé. But from the image of my deathbed, I have learned the frightening degree of deception of which my false self is capable. I have seen how small pets and projects can become life-robbing idols. I know my only hope is in the truth God whispers about my significance to him and the security of his love. Each day I am learning to whisper "As you wish" to God and to my wife and daughters, and each time I do, a life-giving seed is planted. A new garden is growing that is choking out the Audrey IIs.

TREATMENT FOR A FALSE SELF

I have found that we can do some things to unseat the false self and keep ourselves more connected to God. If we spend time with him, practice his presence, believe in his kingdom, and learn from him, we will both love and become more like him. And the character of Christ is the very nature of our true self.

Self-Assessment

The first step in unseating a false self is identifying it in your life. As you read the following list of characteristics, check off all that apply to you. Think about how you experience this on a daily basis and the impact it has on your relationship with God and others.

1. I am more aware of what I want to do with my life than what God wants me to do.
2. I rarely think about how God is involved in the mundane affairs of my life.
3. God has better things to do with his time than hang out with me all day.
✓4. I am often critical of others or myself when it feels that my goals are not being met.
5. My thoughts often turn to anxious preoccupations about the future.
6. I often feel like I am playing a role or wearing a mask when I'm with others.
7. I frequently catch myself making comparisons to others to determine if I am ahead or behind them in some area of life.
8. If I could do a better job of controlling my circumstances, I would be happier.
9. I often wonder what others are thinking about me.
10. I believe God is judgmental and that I have to do the right things to win his approval.
11. My relationship with God feels more distant than intimate.
12. I'm not sure I can completely trust God to have my best interests at heart.

If you checked more than a couple of those statements, keep reading.

Unless we are attentive, the temperature of our soul, the flame of our initial love for Christ, can die down and the embers grow cold. To keep the soul molten and put the true self back in its rightful place, consider the following suggestions.

Letting Go of Self-Rule: Purgation

Purgation refers to the purification of one's character through confession of sin and adoption of an attitude of detachment from worldly possessions and values. It is letting go of beliefs, attitudes, and behaviors that pull us away from relationship with God. In the stage of purgation, we weep bitter tears as we become aware of the costs of self-rule and resolve to stand up from our pigpen and head back home.

Identify and renounce all our God-substitutes (renunciation). The most common idols include: various possessions, alternative life-giving relationships, social status, career, a philosophy of life other than what was set forth by Jesus in the Sermon on the Mount. Gray Temple[4] suggests that we can identify these by completing the following sentence: If Jesus disappoints me, I can always...

Be accountable to at least one person (accountability). This person should care more about the state of your soul than your opinion of him or her. Be completely honest with this person about your internal battleground and tendency to become dependent on substitutes for God. Allow this person to ask you, "Have you returned to use any of your idols this week?"

Make a list of some things you know you should be doing to foster conversation and communion with God, and do them (obedience). Give your accountability partner a copy of the list, and encourage him or her to ask if you have been doing the things you know to do.

Seeing the Glorious Possibilities: Illumination

Illumination refers to a growing personal experience of God's love and peace and an increasing willingness to surrender one's will to God. It is built on openness and honesty before God and an increasing desire for and enjoyment of his transforming presence. This stage is characterized by our becoming dispassionate for all things not God and passionately attached to God and his kingdom. Here, conversations with God increase and begin to deepen into communion and movement toward unceasing prayer/longings from the heart.

For the prodigal, illumination describes the time of staring into the eyes of the Father, seeing the light of pure love in his eyes, and becoming lost in his embrace. Here are some ways we can enhance our ability to defeat our fear of commitment.

Conversation with Christ. Meet with Jesus on a regular basis for conversation. Believe that he is truly present with you, assuming the theological truth that he inhabits the space all around you. Assume also that you are loved without measure.

In your conversation with Jesus be completely transparent. Give him an assessment of the state of your soul, even it means tattling on your false self. Be so bold as to tell him that you do not currently delight in his presence and have doubts about his ability to meet your needs. In the process of dethroning the false self, there are no substitutes for spending time with God and raw honesty.

Don't forget that conversation also includes listening. After speaking your mind, take some time to quiet yourself and become centered. Then become receptive to anything God wants to say. Don't be surprised if he bends your ear about how special you are to him.

Conversation with Scripture. After many aborted plans to read the Bible through in a year, I eventually discovered that it is much more important to get Scripture all the way through me than to get me all the way through Scripture. To help our true self in its battle with our false self, we need to drink deeply from key passages of the Bible that discuss God's love and acceptance. Spend fifteen to thirty minutes each day doing slow, meditative reading from just one passage. Here are some examples of texts that proclaim God's love and care.

- *Psalm 23.* When we allow the Lord to be our shepherd and stay by his side, we experience that we are so cared for we can learn to live without want and trust that our souls will be restored.
- *Psalm 91.* The Lord will cover us with his wings; we are safe in his care; his faithfulness will protect us.
- *Luke 11:1-13.* Contains the Lord's Prayer with its invitation to call

God "Abba" or "Daddy." Also informs us that God's love for us is greater than any parents' love for their children.

- *Luke 12:22-34.* Considering how much we are loved by God helps us resist anxious living.
- *Romans 8:31-39.* Since God is for us, no one can thwart his plans.

Worship the triune God. Since we always come to imitate those we admire, to worship God is to become like God. To worship him means *admiring* the community of love that is the Trinity and becoming swept up in the experience of God's presence with us. While worship is for God's benefit, it is also for ours. It is a crucial mechanism for restoring us to the divine image since it always leaves the soul molten.

Perfect Love Casts out Fear

Only God can expose the false self and its deceitful desires, and remove it from its dominant place in our life. But we must play a part. The best way to unseat the false self is to stay close to God in a posture of openness and raw honesty. Our greatest source of strength may simply be this: God's perfect love can expand and push aside our imperfect fear.

Bible Study: Fear and Love

Text: 1 John 4:12-18; 2 Timothy 1:7, KJV

No one has ever seen God; but if we love one another, God lives in us and his love is made complete in us.

We know that we live in him and he in us, because he has given us of his Spirit. And we have seen and testify that the Father has sent his Son to be the Savior of the world. If anyone acknowledges that Jesus is the Son of God, God lives in him and he in God. And so we know and rely on the love God has for us.

God is love. Whoever lives in love lives in God, and God in him. In this way, love is made complete among us so that we will have confidence on the day of judgment, because in this world we are like him. There is no fear in love. But perfect love drives out fear, because fear has to do with punishment. The one who fears is not made perfect in love.

For God hath not given us the spirit of fear; but of power, and of love, and of a sound mind.

Observations

In the beginning of the Twenty-third Psalm we find the willing words, "The LORD is my shepherd," and in his most famous prayer, immediately after greeting his Father, Jesus says, "Your kingdom come, your will be done" (Matthew 6:10). Surrender ushers us into communion with God. It is the passage between conversation and union. But to surrender is to lay down one's shield and sword; it is to become vulnerable and at the mercy of another. Surrender is necessary before we can enjoy true communion with God—honesty and vulnerability are prerequisites to intimate fellowship. Surrender also brings us face to face with the two competing forces in the universe: the love of God and the fear inherent in original sin.

The passages quoted above from 1 John and 2 Timothy encourage us to stay on the path that leads to union. Both of these apprentices remind us that fear and love cannot occupy the same space, and both encourage us to remain willing and vulnerable before God until his love flushes out the lie that is fear.

Reflection Questions

1. What are some of the ways in which you acknowledge Jesus as the Son of God? (See 1 John 4:15.)
2. What are the practical realities of having Christ *in* you?
3. How does knowing that the essence of God is love change the way you live?
4. How is it that perfect love can drive out fear from your life? Can perfect fear drive out love?

Meditation: Attending Your Own Funeral

Explanation

The following meditation can help you become aware of ways in which the presence of fears and idols may be preventing you from enjoying life with God and others to the fullest.

Meditation

After taking yourself through the Five Ps of Prayer, go through the following exercise. You may wish to read it through several times and then move through the movements from memory. Or you may prefer to simply pause after you read each sentence to visualize (and "hear") whatever is suggested by each phrase.

- Imagine that you see your body in a coffin and laid out in a church for your funeral rites. Take a good look at your body, especially at the expression on your face.
- Now look at all the people who have come to your funeral. Go slowly from one pew to another, looking at the faces of these people. Stop before each person and see what he is thinking and feeling. Pay close attention especially to your spouse, children, immediate family members, and closest friends.

- Now listen to the sermon that is being preached. Who is the preacher? What is he saying about you? Can you accept all the good things he is saying about you? If you cannot, notice what resistances there are in you to accepting what the preacher is saying. Which of the good things he says about you are you willing to accept? How do you feel when you hear him speak?

- Look again at the faces of your friends who are attending your funeral. Imagine all the good things they will be saying about you when they return home from your funeral. What do you feel now? Is there something you would like to say to each of them before they go home? Some final farewell in response to all they are thinking and feeling about you? Say it and see what this does to you.

- Imagine that the funeral rites are over. You stand above the grave in which your body lies, watching your friends leave the cemetery. What are your feelings now? Look back on your life and your experiences. Was it all worthwhile? How would you summarize your life?

- Now become aware of your existence here in the room, and realize that you are still alive and still have some time at your disposal. Think of these same friends from your present point of view. Do you see them differently as a result of this exercise? Think of yourself. Do you see yourself differently or feel differently about yourself as a result of this exercise? Are there any ways that fear or idols caused you to live in ways you regret? What can you do to change the course of the rest of your life?

Spiritual Exercise: Foundational Experience

Brief Background

Everyone has a drive for pleasure, significance, and security. While each of these needs can best be met through a relationship with Christ, sometimes fear that these desires will be unfulfilled and idols (God-substitutes for satisfying these desires) pull us away from finding fulfillment in Christ. The following exercise allows you to consider the impact of your fears and idols on the pursuit of these three goals.

Exercise

Meditate on each of the following human drives while considering any ways you have pursued satisfaction of these needs apart from God.

- *Pleasure* (how I can be gratified). Consider all the ways you have pursued pleasure in ways you know are outside the bounds of God's intention for you. Pray for help in letting go of these idols.
- *Significance* (what others think of me). Consider how you have invested time in pursuing the favorable opinion of others in ways that took you away from spending time with God and others. Pray for forgiveness and insight into where your significance is found.
- *Security* (what I have and what I do). Name five sources of security for you apart from God's promises. Pray for an infusion of divine love that will drown all fear and take away your need for security apart from your daily renewed relationship with God.

Chapter 7

Surrender Hurts

The Sweet Ache of Letting Go

When Christ calls a man, he bids him come and die.

DIETRICH BONHOEFFER

If anyone would come after me, he must deny himself and take up his cross and follow me. For whoever wants to save his life will lose it, but whoever loses his life for me will find it.

MATTHEW 16:24-25

Let's not talk about love. Let's not sing about love. Let's put love into action and make it real.

CLARENCE JORDAN

Clarence Jordan was ahead of his time. A product of the Deep South, he brought Scripture to life with a modern-day southern translation of the New Testament, *The Cotton Patch Gospel.* It was *The Message* with a twang.

In 1942, at age thirty, Clarence moved to Sumter County, near Americus, Georgia, to live out the teachings of Jesus amid the poverty and racism of that area. He founded Koinonia Farm as a pioneering interracial community where blacks and whites could live and work side by side, in the spirit of New Testament kinship.

The community met with local opposition in the early fifties. A specific crisis came when they were having trouble getting LP gas delivered for heating during the winter, even though it was against the law not to deliver gas. Apparently the local gas supplier didn't approve of what Clarence was attempting to model.[1]

Clarence approached his brother Robert (later a state senator and justice of the Georgia Supreme Court) to ask him to provide legal representation for Koinonia Farm. Clarence thought Robert could do something through a phone call. However, Robert responded, "Clarence, I can't do that. You know my political aspirations. Why, if I represent you, I might lose my job, my house, everything I've got."

"We might lose everything too, Bob."

"It's different for you."

"Why is it different? I remember, it seems to me, that you and I joined the church on the same Sunday, as boys. I expect, when we came forward, the preacher asked me about the same question he did you. He asked me, 'Do you accept Jesus as your Lord and Savior.' And I said, 'Yes.' What did you say?"

"I follow Jesus, Clarence, up to a point."

"Could that point by any chance be—the cross?"

"That's right. I follow him to the cross, but not *on* the cross. I'm not getting myself crucified."

"Then I don't believe you're a disciple. You're an admirer of Jesus, but not a disciple of his. I think you ought to go back to the church you belong to and tell them you're an admirer, not a disciple."

"Well, now, if everyone who felt like I do did that, we wouldn't *have* a church, would we?"

"The question is," Clarence said, "'Do you have a church?'"

Clarence's question sounds a lot like the question asked at the beginning of this book: If Jesus came to turn our world right-side up, why do so many of his followers continue to live such upside-down lives?

While I can only speculate for the masses, I can answer that question for myself. I have spent most of my life as what Dallas Willard calls a vampire Christian. I have wanted just enough of the blood of Christ to have eternal life but not the full transfusion that would make me into a new creature, living life in a perpetual state of "As you wish." My desire to live as ruler in my own realm of influence gets in the way of my desire to live life in God's kingdom. I willingly follow Jesus up to the cross and admire his love, but my false self resists following him onto the cross and participating in his example of absolute surrender. Give me the fire insurance policy. Keep the Refiner's fire.

Fortunately I have more to me than a false self. The truest part of me wants a total restoration of relationship with God—conversation, communion, and union. That part knows this will only happen in full, and life will only become abundant, if I *cherish* the cross of Christ and *accept* my own personal cross.

The Cross of Christ

More than any other symbol, the cross represents the Christian faith. The cross, empty tomb, and the communion chalice rest at the heart and soul of Christianity. On the cross Jesus demonstrated radical willingness and obedience to his Father's will. In Christ's acceptance of death on the cross, he modeled for us that nothing, not our deepest fears or our most cherished idols, can come between God and us. Our heart must be like his: dead to this world, alive in the kingdom forever.

The writers of the Synoptic Gospels knew the importance of the cross. In addition to painting graphic word pictures of Jesus' sacrificial death as our means to atonement, each was also careful to quote Jesus' words to his apprentices about the cross they must bear: "If any man will come after me, let him deny himself, and take up his cross, and follow me."[2]

What does this mean? Can't we just overlook that one sentence and continue on our way? Jesus must have anticipated our question. A few chapters later he answers no.

The necessity of putting the false self to death, of taking up the cross, is amplified in Jesus' unsettling encounter with a rich young man.[3] Jesus looks into the face of the would-be apprentice and loves him. Why not? The young man has everything going for him. He is what most pastors and counselors dream of—the perfect YAVIS helpee: *y*oung, *a*rticulate, *v*erbal, *i*ntelligent, and *s*ophisticated. He is also rich and highly motivated—two more very appealing traits. Who wouldn't want to help this fellow and have him as a disciple?

But there is one thing he doesn't have, and Jesus knows it. He says to the man, "One thing you lack.... Go, sell everything you have and give to the poor, and you will have treasure in heaven. Then come, follow me."[4]

At those words the young man's face falls, and he goes away sad. Apparently his false self has made an idol of his wealth, and the young man is not willing to place that part of himself on the cross of surrender.

The Pain of Breaking Free

The invitation to communion with God is a call to radical willingness and surrender. But as we have seen, continuing on this road to union with God brings to light our deepest fears and most cherished idols—none of which can pass through God's screen door. The cross—a symbol of pain, suffering, and ultimate victory—is necessary to mortify our fears and shatter our idols. The cross both empowers us and represents the pain of breaking free.

Many of us are like the rich young man, unwilling to place our idols in the dumpster. We cannot do it on our own. We need God's help, and often that help comes in the form of pain.

The pain of spiritual transformation differs from the pain caused by the presence of evil in the world. That remains, for the most part, a mystery. Sometimes tornadoes touch down in trailer parks and cars hit little children, and mortal minds cannot answer the question why. Sometimes very bad things happen to very good people, and it has nothing to do with personal crosses and the need for character formation.

Victims of the mystery of evil need someone to sit with them, hug them, and offer only love. What helps them most is empathy, not explanation; presence, not preconceptions; tears, not "truth." Those slammed by evil need to believe that a strong and powerful God is offering them the same thing: his presence and his tears. The problem of evil will remain a mystery until we get to heaven.

In contrast, the pain that comes from Christian character formation is a *specific and focused* type of pain. It has an identifiable purpose. God is using the pain to purge our lives of idols and to make us more like his Son. The particular ache of a "personal cross" is always associated with becoming more like Christ and typically exists in one of three forms:

- When we move *away* from God, we will experience the natural and logical consequences of willfulness. Our pain points out our need for God and can prompt us to willing surrender once again.
- When we move *toward* God, sometimes it can suddenly seem that he has vanished. God often uses such "dark night of the soul" experiences to expose our need for deeper and deeper intimacy with him.
- When we move *toward* God and are fully aware of his presence, we can experience the pain of persecution *and* the pain of the Refiner's fire.

MOVING AWAY FROM GOD

Dan was born in east Kansas to poor, hardworking parents. When Dan was seven, his father died and his mother was left alone to raise him and his two older sisters. His mom never made more than ten thousand dollars a year, but somehow she managed to keep her children fed.

Dan was born with what his doctor called a nervous stomach. The less medically inclined might say, "That boy's idle is set too high." He battled fear and anxiety almost every day. He didn't eat very much and was as skinny as straw.

During his teenage years, Dan discovered that illegal drugs would put his fear and anxiety into hibernation for a while. He became a frequent user.

But not too many years passed before he discovered better solutions: Jesus and the care of a good doctor. Reading Scripture about Christ's love for him and meditating on the presence of a twenty-four-hour-a-day friend had a soothing effect on Dan's anxiety. It dialed down his fears and calmed his stomach. Falling in love with Jesus, coupled with the occasional use of antianxiety medication, changed Dan's life.

Dan went off to Bible school and then to seminary. He was a natural academic. At the recommendation of his professors, he applied to a Ph.D. program in theology. He was accepted and learned several languages and read stacks of dusty books.

Dan's primary professor, one of the top evangelical theologians in the world, liked his work and encouraged him to teach in a graduate school. Instead Dan accepted a more humble call and began teaching undergraduates at a little church school in his home state.

To Dan the job was just shy of heaven. The students liked him because he was real and because he would play computer games with them. The administrators liked him because he was smart. They made him head of the department. His church liked him because he was excited about Jesus. They placed him on the board of elders.

But two problems bubbled beneath the surface of Dan's wonderful life: one physical and one spiritual. With the pressures of adult living—a wife, children, and a modest income—Dan's nervous stomach shifted into high gear. But instead of continuing to trust in the care of the Great Physician and their family doctor, Dan decided that he knew best how to treat his problem, and so he drank wine to calm his anxiety.

The switch worked; less anxiety and no side effects. You could almost hear Dan's false self whisper, "I knew I could do a better job than them." But it wasn't long before Dan's way was working too well, and things got out of hand. He loved the feeling of being in control of his anxiety relief and the buzz of intoxication. But unknown to Dan, his father had been a closet alcoholic. Apparently, Dan's genetic makeup was much like his father's. Dan had been a dormant alcoholic. But his condition was inactive no more.

The one drink at night became two, three, then six. Then the six became twelve. In spite of warnings from his wife and a few friends, Dan stayed on the path of self-management. He traveled down the road of willfulness, picking up speed all the while.

A few months later, Dan was driving after he had been drinking. He crossed a median and sideswiped a school bus. Miraculously, no one was seriously injured. But Dan witnessed a nightmare of what almost was that he would never forget. He realized in the bottom of his soul that he had made controlling his emotions the most important thing in his life. He had been doing it without asking either his doctor or God for help because he feared that their suggestions might not provide immediate relief. With sincere humility, he confessed to all what had happened, entered into a treatment center, and placed himself under the care of an Alcoholics Anonymous sponsor and at the mercy of his superiors. He said he would do anything to make things right with anyone who had been hurt by his actions. While acknowledging he didn't deserve mercy, he asked for mercy.

God graciously answered Dan's plea. He began to show up again for conversation. God used Dan's experience of traveling away from willingness to expose his fear that God cannot be trusted and his dependency on control and self-management.

While Dan still had his "high idle," he chose to turn around and begin moving toward God again. He turned in the keys to his private kingdom of self-control and embraced the cross of true freedom, placing his will on the beams. Surrender and honesty reestablished deep communion between Dan and God.

DARK NIGHTS OF THE SOUL

Dan's pain makes sense. After all, if we keep acting like a donkey, we may grow ears, and if we are lucky, the pain of donkey-doom serves as a wake-up call to our true self and motivates us to think things through and try a different course.

John of the Cross, though, described a more puzzling type of pain. It's a pain that occurs even as we are moving *toward* God. It's the pain of his perceived absence—even as it seems we are doing all the right things.

John of the Cross was born in Fantiveros, Castile, in Spain, about fifty years after Columbus sailed east, and he died in 1591. Between those two dates, John became a Carmelite monk, studied philosophy and theology at one of Europe's leading universities, developed a friendship with Teresa of Avila, and gave spiritual theology some new vocabulary.

John was put in charge of his order and showed keen leadership abilities. As a result of both his suffering and commitment, he was named John of the Cross. He became committed to Catholic reform and was outspoken about this need in his writings. Eventually he was arrested and put in confinement by the church leadership, which opposed the reform. During his time of imprisonment, he wrote his most famous book, *The Dark Night of the Soul*.

In that work John described the work of God upon the soul—not through joy and light, but through sorrow and darkness. His concept of "dark nights" has become an integral part of understanding the journey to intimacy and union with God.

It's common today for people to misuse the label "dark night." The deep ache of grief after the death of a loved one, for instance, is not what John of the Cross meant by a "dark night of the soul" experience. Also, when people lose interest in pleasure and live their lives under a cloud of despair and sadness, it does not mean they are having a "dark night" experience. They may be experiencing an episode of major depression and be in need of medication. While God can redeem these situations, he did not necessarily induce the dark emotions. They have nothing to do with soul transformation.

The "dark night" experience described by John of the Cross refers to the loss of the pleasure we once experienced in our devotional life. For a period of time it's as if God quits showing up for times of expected conversation and communion. But God does this because he wants to purify us and move us to greater spiritual heights.

After conversion, according to John of the Cross, it seems that our soul is

Saint John of the Cross

According to John of the Cross, "dark night" experiences often expose the following idols:

Spiritual pride: becoming too spiritual to be of earthly good

Spiritual greed: being more attached to spiritual feelings than to God

Spiritual luxury: substituting sensual substitutes for spiritual pleasure

Spiritual wrath: lack of patience with the journey of transformation

Spiritual gluttony: trying to subdue the flesh by our own will and effort

Spiritual envy: desire for praise for spiritual growth

Spiritual sloth: becoming weary of spiritual exercises and the pursuit of God "nurtured and caressed by the Spirit." He observed, "Like a loving mother, God cares for and comforts the infant soul by feeding it spiritual milk."[5] This stage in our relationship with God brings great delight and joy. In the imagery of Psalm 23, the pastures are green and the water, still and cool. But God does not want us to rest there forever. He also wants to restore the soul to health, vitality, and union with himself. This restoration may require rearrangements and even surgery.

A restored soul will come to be characterized more by love than fear. God, not idols of significance and security, will be present in the soul's Holy of Holies. There comes a time in our journey back to God's house where he bids us to grow deeper, to become purer. Again, to use John's words, "He will remove the previous consolation from the soul in order to teach it virtue and prevent it from developing vice."[6]

All believers who want to become an apprentice of Christ and not just his admirer will find themselves in the blank space between the verses in Psalm 23. Because he loves us so much, the Shepherd moves on. We look around and wonder where he has gone. We feel alone, abandoned. We call out. Nothing. The voice that used to call our name is silent and does not respond when we call. He is gone. He has moved farther down the road that leads home. During the dark night experience our job is to seek God and to go to him again. When we do, we will realize that we are not the same person. Our relationship with him is not the same. We have moved. We are closer to home and closer to union.

That's what Jan discovered.

Jan was a cradle Christian. Half of her coloring books had pictures of Jesus in them. She had so many perfect-attendance pins from Sunday school it was difficult for her to hold her shoulders back when she walked. She went to a private Christian high school and then to a Christian college. At some point during her sophomore year, she got zapped by the Holy Spirit and began speaking in tongues. Her soul was on fire. She loved the feeling of being lost in God.

Jan wanted more of that feeling. She wanted to be, in her words, "wherever a fresh wind of God is blowing." Her life began to revolve around attending revival services, spending time with prayer partners, and listening to worship music.

She also hit the road. When she heard about a special "outpouring," she was off to be a part of it. When she read about a long-lasting revival at a church in Florida, she made sure her spring break was spent on the front row. Jan loved the feelings of worship.

Then one day the special feelings stopped. She went to her quiet time with God and felt that she was alone. She went to church and felt nothing. She prayed and it felt as if she were talking to herself. Where had he gone? Why were the ceilings brass?

After about a month, she asked God what was going on, and to her surprise, he showed up and whispered something important in her ear. *Child, I love you so much. But you were beginning to become more attached to your feelings than to me.*

That was all it took. Jan realized that she had become so fixated on the gifts of God that she had all but forgotten the Giver. Her dark month of being less aware of God's presence was like smelling salts, awakening her to the main thing: loving God. She also began to relax in the fact the she didn't have to go anywhere to be in the center of God's presence.

In "dark night" experiences God uses the pain and suffering associated with his absence to expose our need for deeper and deeper levels of communion with him. These times prepare the soul for the next movement—union.

THE PAIN OF IMITATING CHRIST

We can experience pain as we are moving *away* from God and as we are journeying *toward* God when it seems that he is absent for a time. We can also experience a personal cross even when we feel God's presence in our lives. That's what

Communion

Clarence Jordan, the farmer-theologian at the beginning of this chapter, experienced. Clarence had a heart like Christ's. He embraced radical willingness, saying "As you wish," despite intense pressure and great personal cost.

Because of its opposition to what he was doing with Koinonia Farm, the church that Clarence led in worship and where his wife, Florence, had taught Sunday school, excommunicated the couple in the name of Jesus. Apparently the deacons wanted the Golden Rule taught in separate Sunday schools.

The persecution got worse. Violence against Koinonia Farm escalated. Angry neighbors chopped down nearly three hundred fruit trees, stole crops, and dumped garbage on the property. The Ku Klux Klan got involved with intimidation that included bullets and burning crosses. During a shooting attack, Clarence took his Bible and a wooden chair and sat under a yard light. He later said that he wanted to be sure the KKK shot the right person and not one of the children.

Clarence's maturation in reflecting the image of Christ, however, did not happen in the twinkling of an eye. Nor did it happen apart from the acceptance of his personal cross. On March 13, 1959, he wrote a letter that reflects his inner thoughts during the time his community was under attack.

> I remember the night Harry Atkinson and I were on our way over
> to the roadside market after we had received word that it had been
> bombed and was burning. When we came over the hill we could see the
> fiery glow on the horizon, and this ignited a burning in my heart. I was
> scorched with anger, and I'm sure if I had known who had committed
> the act, there would have been considerable hatred in my heart. At that
> time I doubt that I could have distinguished between anger and hate.
>
> But as I had occasion to think, I realized that the hate was rooted in
> a consuming possessiveness. True, I had given up personal possessions,
> only to find that I had transplanted it from an individual to a group
> basis. The market was our property; together we sweated to build it; and

now it was burning, and I was too. The damned culprits have destroyed our property, I thought. And I hated their guts. Later I had the same reaction when various ones, including myself and my children, were shot at. The so-and-so's were trying to take our lives from us.

The solution to this soul-destroying condition came only upon the recognition that neither property nor lives were ours but God's. They never had really been ours in any sense of the word. We hadn't even "given them back to Him"—they were His all along. And if this was the way He wanted to spend His property and His people in order to accomplish His purposes, why should we pitch a tantrum?[7]

Over time Clarence Jordan learned to bear the cross of Christ in a gentle manner that transformed his life and served as a consistent reminder of the cost of apprenticeship. He discovered the meaning of what Dietrich Bonhoeffer called renunciation. Unless one is willing to renounce fame, prestige, and the quest for fortune and popularity, one cannot fully follow Christ. Jordan, like Bonhoeffer, saw clearly the impossibility of fully sharing Christ's resurrection without being willing to share fully in his crucifixion.

Am I saying that a person has to be as detached from the world as Clarence Jordan or Bonhoeffer before considering himself to be a Christian? Certainly not. But I am suggesting that arising to the Easter abundance of deep union with Christ does depend on our willingness to accept our personal cross, to have our will become one with God's. Because of his desire to be like Jesus, Clarence Jordan accepted the pain of the Refiner's fire. He became willing for God to incinerate any part of his character that could not be united with God.

NECESSARY BUT TEMPORARY

Moving into deeper levels of intimate fellowship with God requires that we become completely real with him about the state of our heart. Is it willing and pliable in his hands, or has it become willful and rigid? When we honestly answer this question, we discover the extent to which our fears and idols interfere with the experience of communion with God, and we hear his whispered solution: *Accept the sweet ache of letting go, the pain of your personal cross.*

Our role during these times is simply to trust the Surgeon and stay on the operating table. Each time we awake from these soul surgeries, we will see both the world and kingdom more clearly and find that our heart has expanded and now pulses with even more of the love and joy of Christ. We will discover how the experience of true communion creates an insatiable appetite for consummation.

~~~~~

Bible Study: Rich Young Ruler

Text: Mark 10:17-21, KJV; Matthew 16:24-26;
Galatians 6:14

> And when he was gone forth into the way, there came one running, and kneeled to him, and asked him, Good Master, what shall I do that I may inherit eternal life? And Jesus said unto him, Why callest thou me good? there is none good but one, that is, God. Thou knowest the commandments, Do not commit adultery, Do not kill, Do not steal, Do not bear false witness, Defraud not, Honour thy father and mother. And he answered and said unto him, Master, all these have I observed from my youth. Then Jesus beholding him loved him, and said unto him, One thing thou lackest: go thy way, sell whatsoever thou hast, and give to the

poor, and thou shalt have treasure in heaven: and come, take up the cross, and follow me.

Then Jesus said to his disciples, "If anyone would come after me, he must deny himself and take up his cross and follow me. For whoever wants to save his life will lose it, but whoever loses his life for me will find it. What good will it be for a man if he gains the whole world, yet forfeits his soul? Or what can a man give in exchange for his soul?

May I never boast except in the cross of our Lord Jesus Christ, through which the world has been crucified to me, and I to the world.

Observations

A rich young man approaches Jesus and asks how he might *earn* eternal life. Jesus seems to ignore his question and asks one of his own, and his question reveals the answer to the man's initial question. Jesus forces the young man to consider that his only hope is in total dependence on God, who alone can give eternal life. Jesus also identifies himself with God.

When Jesus begins to list the Ten Commandments, the young man interrupts before Jesus can finish the list and declares that he has kept them all since he was a boy. But he does not realize the difference between external conformity (which does not require internal transformation) and internal conformity (which does).

Jesus loves the young man so much that he goes to the heart of the matter: the young man's heart. He tells him to do something that will require a total renovation of his heart and a movement into the land of no fear and no idols. In giving away his wealth, the young man would remove the idol that keeps him from trusting Jesus. But he can't.

This story poignantly illustrates how easy it is to allow our fears and idols—and our desire to avoid the pain of facing life without them—to keep us on the wrong side of our personal cross. For more than two thousand years this story has challenged all admirers of Jesus to trust him enough to accept our personal cross and become his apprentices.

Reflection Questions

1. Do you think Jesus' admonition to sell everything you have and give to the poor is meant for all Christians, or is it targeted to those who use money as an idol for pleasure, esteem, and security?
2. How do you describe the difference between internal and external conformity?
3. In your own words, explain Matthew 16:24-26 to the rich young ruler.
4. Do the same with Galatians 6:14.

Meditation: Raising All Four Flags

Explanation

The great enemies of a transformed will are duplicity (wanting to eat from both trees in the garden), deceitfulness (lying about having eaten from both trees), and darkness (running from God's presence to hide in shame).

Dallas Willard proposes a four-part solution—four steps in the progression toward complete identification of our will with God's. These steps are effective ways to battle duplicity, deceit, and darkness.

It is suggested that you practice the discipline of silence for at least five minutes as you ask God in prayer to reveal to you where you are with each of these steps.

Meditation
1. Have I become willing to be made willing? (With this first step I realize that completing this journey is beyond what I can do on my own. The best thing I can do is desire to be made willing.)
2. Have I prayed for your grace and wisdom, Father, to move me to even deeper levels of surrender—ultimately to full abandonment of all that is not you?
3. Have I moved beyond abandonment to find *contentment* with your will? Am I experiencing gratitude and joy as constants in my life?
4. Have I moved beyond contentment to experience energetic *participation* in accomplishing your will, Father? Am I learning to reign—to exercise dominion—as part of your original design in Eden?

Spiritual Exercise: Ignatian Examination of Conscience

Brief Background
The Spiritual Exercises of St. Ignatius contains an exercise known as Examination of Conscience. Typically used at the end of the day, it is a way to keep us accountable to the task of pursuing God and his kingdom.

Exercise: Method of Making the General Examination of Conscience
- Give thanks to God for the favors you have received throughout the day.
- Ask for the grace to know your sins and to free yourself from them. For our purpose, we will specifically focus on the times where we acted out of fear instead of love.

- Demand an account of your soul from the moment of rising until the present examination, either hour by hour or from one period to another. It may be helpful to review the day by blocks of time (before breakfast, between breakfast and lunch, between lunch and the evening meal, and before the end of the day).
- Ask pardon of God our Lord for your failings—particularly with regard to being driven by fear or in the pursuit of idols that distract you from being present to God's love.
- Resolve to amend your life with the help of God's grace.
- Close the exercise with a "breathed" Lord's Prayer.

Living Out of the Divine Center

Thomas R. Kelly

With this chapter we complete our discussion of the second of the three movements of transformation—communion. Just as the key ingredient to conversation with God is *time,* communion with God is built on the central component of *honesty,* even when what is in our hearts conflicts with what God desires for us.

Do you ever feel torn between conflicting desires? A part of you longs for deeper intimacy with God, to enjoy his fellowship and live your life connected to his love. But another element of you, the secretly ambitious part, has other ideas. Its focus is external; its desire is for validation and the praise of others. Communion versus competition. Which road do you take?

A man who wrestled with this question was Thomas Raymond Kelly.[8] Born to hardworking Quaker parents on June 4, 1893, on a farm in southwestern Ohio, Kelly experienced hardship early in life. Before Kelly's fifth birthday, his father died and his mother had to work the farm alone to make ends meet.

Even though she was busy with manual labor, his mother noticed that Thomas was intellectually gifted. She did all she could to support his education, sacrificing greatly to make sure he was able to attend college.

Thomas began his academic career at Wilmington College and took to academic life, well, like a Quaker takes to silence. He majored in chemistry and became a lab rat. But that changed when he decided to go to Haverford College for his senior year and discovered philosophy.

For the next twenty-two years Thomas Kelly devoted himself to academic pursuits and the quest to uncover the meaning of life. But duplicity tore at the center of his soul. His heart wanted to go in two different directions.

Part of him wanted the stamp of approval of a prestigious university. He idolized the philosophy department at Harvard University and hoped they would write an A+ on his forehead. His eyes were always on the Ivy League prize.

He was tantalizingly close to his goal in 1930. He filled a one-year vacancy at Wellesley College so that he could also spend time studying at Harvard. But he paid a very high price for touching greatness. He sacrificed finances and family time to pursue his dream of hearing an "attaboy" from the raters and grade-givers at Harvard.

But his heart was also pulled toward God. He also spent much of his life on altruistic acts, including doing volunteer work among German prisoners of war and revitalizing a Quaker study center. As he said to his mentor, Rufus Jones, "I'm just going to make my life a miracle."[9]

Thomas Kelly wanted both acclaim and communion.

It wasn't until he finally got his book published in 1937—the crescendo point to seven years of sacrifice—that the fissure in his torn soul began to heal.

In late autumn of 1937, Kelly's life took a new direction. He was forty-four. The strained period of duplicity was finally over. While he would live only three more years, what he discovered in silent listening prayer was the pathway to communion with God. It changed his life and the lives of countless others who have discovered his words.

People first noticed the difference in Kelly when he addressed Quaker meetings. It's said that he suddenly began to speak differently and with great authenticity. Something important had dropped from his head to his heart. He was expounding less as one possessed with knowledge about God and more as one who had an unmistakable acquaintance with God.[10]

We don't know if there was a precise moment when the light bulb turned on, but through Kelly's lectures we know that he began to enjoy communion with God that was both holy and sweet. Listen to his words below, collected under the themes that relate to the process of experiencing intimate fellowship with God.

Communion with God Is Available to All

[All are called] to the practice of orienting their entire being in inward adoration about the springs of immediacy and ever-fresh divine power.[11]

In His graciousness God gives us His gifts, even in intermittent communion, and touches us into flame…but the hunger of the committed one is for unbroken communion and adoration.[12]

Communion Requires the Surrender of the Will

The crux of religious living lies in the will, not in transient and variable states…. Where the will to will God's will is present, there is a child of God.[13]

It is to one strand in this inner dream, one scene, where the Shepherd has found His sheep, that I would direct you. It is the life of absolute and complete and holy obedience to the voice of the Shepherd.[14]

Communion Requires Honesty About Our Duplicity

Double-mindedness in this matter is wholly destructive of the spiritual life…. Unless the willingness is present to be stripped of our last earthly dignity and hope and yet still praise Him, we have no message in this our day of refugees, bodily and spiritual.[15]

There are plenty to follow our Lord half-way, but not the other half. They will give up possessions, friends and honors, but it touches them too closely to disown themselves.[16]

Communion Requires an Acceptance of the Cross

Paradoxically, this total instruction proceeds in two opposing directions at once.... He plucks the world out of our hearts, loosening the chains of attachment. And then he hurls the world into our hearts.[17]

The Cross as dogma is painless speculation; the Cross as lived suffering is anguish and glory. Yet God, out of the pattern of his own heart, has planted the Cross along the road of holy obedience. And He enacts in the hearts *of those he loves the miracle of willingness to welcome suffering and to know it for what it is—the final seal of his gracious love.*[18]

The Results Are Extraordinary

A soul is in Other whose life is our true life, whose love is our love, whose joy is our joy, whose peace is our peace, whose burdens are our burdens and whose will is our will.[19]

The last mark of this simplified life is radiant joy.[20]

The image of Jacob wrestling with an angel was a metaphor for how Thomas Kelly had lived most of his life—resisting surrender to divine will. But three years before he died, he gave up and let the angel win. With the few years he had left, he traveled and lectured about the journey to communion with God that he had traveled. He found it to be a path of *willingness, honesty about the warring nature of his two selves—true and false,* and the *acceptance of his personal cross.* His life story celebrates communion with God and whets the appetite for progressively deeper levels of union.

Part 3

Consummation

Christ Incarnate
in Me

Chapter 8

Forgiveness

The Importance of Staying Connected to Love

> *Forgiveness is the key that can unshackle us from a past that will not rest in the grave of things over and done with. As long as our minds are captive to the memory of having been wronged, they are not free to wish for reconciliation.*
>
> LEWIS B. SMEDES

> *Where there is hatred, let me sow love, were there is injury, pardon.... For it is in giving that we receive, it is in pardoning that we are pardoned.*
>
> SAINT FRANCIS OF ASSISI

Imagine your pastor telling the congregation on Sunday morning, "I know you've got those tithe checks half written, but if you can think of someone with whom you have fallen out of relationship—even if it's not your fault—put your checkbook away. Don't even stay around for my sermon. Go and restore your broken relationship. It's the most important thing you can do."

Yet Jesus places such an importance on forgiveness and the resolution of conflict that he says even if we are in the process of offering a gift in church we should leave immediately if we, at that moment, remember someone who has something against us. "Leave your gift there in front of the altar. First go and be reconciled to your brother; then come and offer your gift" (Matthew 5:24).

According to Jesus, forgiveness is a central, reciprocal, and fundamental part of Christian living. He says it's so important to relationships that its practice should be limitless. We are to offer forgiveness an infinite number of times (see Matthew 18:21-22). Even as he hung from the cross, his body exploding in pain, Jesus' final words were the gift of forgiveness to those who were responsible for his torture and death: "Father, forgive them, for they do not know what they are doing" (Luke 23:34).

Why? Why was forgiveness so important to Jesus? Because he knew that forgiveness makes it possible for us to love others as ourselves as well as God with our whole heart.

WHY FORGIVE?

Jesus was a great summarizer. When one of the Pharisees tested him with the question, "Teacher, which is the greatest commandment in the Law?" (Matthew 22:36), Jesus was able to do a quick survey of the more than seven hundred injunctions and go to the heart of the matter. " 'Love the Lord your God with all your heart and with all your soul and with all your mind,' " he said, adding, "This is the first and greatest commandment. And the second is like it: 'Love your neighbor as yourself.' All the Law and the Prophets hang on these two commandments" (Matthew 22:37-40).

Later, during his commencement address to his followers, he reminded them of the same principle: nothing is more important than love. "My command is this: Love each other as I have loved you. Greater love has no one than this, that he lay down his life for his friends" (John 15:12-13).

But unforgiveness clogs the heart with hurt, anger, and resentment and restricts the nourishing flow of love. That's what it did to John.

John and Helen were deeply in love. Everyone said they would get married. But John kept finding reasons to put off popping the question. Then Pearl Harbor exploded, and he was drafted into service.

As John was about to step onto the bus that would take him to boot camp, he desperately wanted to ask Helen to marry him. They could find a preacher after his initial weeks of push-ups and marching.

But he couldn't bear the idea of leaving her a war widow. The words stayed in his throat as he kissed her good-bye. Deep inside himself, he made a vow. "If I make it through this war alive, she'll be my wife."

John was away for almost three years. During that time Helen began to have misgivings about his intentions. After all, he had never put them into words. She loved John very much, but doubts about his love for her began to grow like ragweed in her heart. As the months turned into years, these fears choked out her hope of ever enjoying a life with John.

Helen's dilemma wasn't helped by the fact that John didn't write. Was he conducting a strange test of Helen's love, of God's faithfulness? No one knows. But sadly, when Johnny finally came marching home, three years to the week after he left, he found Helen married to his best friend.

John's hurt was an ocean. How his skin managed to contain the tides was a great mystery, but the waves of his despair were obvious to all. He never forgave Helen or Ray, his best friend.

John lived with the destructive forces of unforgiveness for more than half a century. The weight of it eventually stooped his posture and pulled at his face. No one can remember ever seeing him smile. But most sadly, unforgiveness turned his soul to stone. He became a cold loner who critiqued God and the universe with cynical reviews.

John spent the next fifty years in bitter misery. His pain was magnified by the fact that he never moved away. No one knew why—perhaps some secret hope that Helen would divorce Ray. John lived and worked within a few hundred yards of Helen's new house. He spent each Sunday morning and Wednesday evening sitting in the same church where he had sat beside her, where she now sat with his former friend. During each worship service, his face was a chiseled monument to his grief.

From the painful perch of a church pew, John watched Helen's hair turn gray and the baptisms and marriages of each of her children, wondering, perhaps, how his life would've been different if he had asked her to marry him before stepping on that bus.

What a tragic story! But what made John's heartbreak much worse was his refusal to take the only medicine that could cure it—forgiveness. Maybe John was trying to use his misery to coerce God into stepping in to rewrite his life. If so, his plan didn't work. As the years rolled by, John's unforgiveness closed his heart and kept the healing love of God from rushing in.

John missed more than a life with Helen; he missed life. His bitterness pushed him off the path of conversation, communion, and union with God and into a private pit of despair. Even though he sat in church each week, the door to his heart was bolted from the inside. He came to prefer the perverse pleasure of punishing God to spending time with him as a counselor and friend. While technically a Christian, because of unforgiveness, John's character was never transformed. He never experienced the love, peace, and joy of Christian living. He sat in the presence of God's love each week, but instead of swimming in that ocean, he chose instead to swim in his ocean of bitterness.

John's story is extreme, but it is also true. To some degree many of us insist on holding on to the hot, burning coals of bitterness. But as long as we do, it will bar us from a romantic union with God. Falling for God is a matter of learning to live with him in love and union. Unforgiveness causes us to let go of his hand.

What does love have to do with forgiveness? Everything. As John experienced, anger, hurt, and bitterness, all bound together by unforgiveness, become the deadly plaque that clogs our spiritual arteries. Unforgiveness, which literally means not being willing to give wholly, blocks the flow of love between my neighbor and me, and between God and me. I can no more be simultaneously up and down than I can live in a state of unforgiveness with anyone and keep either of Christ's supreme commandments. If I cannot forgive, I cannot love. Love is the first fruit of the Spirit referenced by Paul in Galatians 5:22. Love will not grow from the soil of a heart made arid by bitterness. If I cannot love, I cannot continue the journey to union with God.

Our ultimate goal of *union* has to do with an overall and complete harmony between God and us. We must surrender our will and allow his Spirit to become ours. Unforgiveness kills union because it forms an impermeable barrier to the free flow of love that is to characterize Christian life.

Listen again to Jesus' words:

Remain in me, and I will remain in you. No branch can bear fruit by itself; it must remain in the vine. Neither can you bear fruit unless you remain in me. (John 15:4)

…that all of them may be one, Father, just as you are in me and I am in you. May they also be in us so that the world may believe that you have sent me. (John 17:21)

In giving in to bitterness and unforgiveness, we unwittingly clog our connection to God, making union impossible. Instead of having the supreme commandments as the foundation of our Christian walk, they become a ceiling we can never reach.

BECOMING LESS MISERABLE

I have a friend—also from the rural South—who became so frustrated trying to pronounce his favorite musical, *Les Misérables,* that he gave up and began calling it "less miserable." Not a bad substitute.

The musical *Les Misérables,* based on the novel by Victor Hugo, eloquently illustrates how forgiveness melts the heart to love. As you may recall, Jean

Valjean, the central character, has been in prison for nineteen years because he stole a loaf of bread for his hungry family. He is out on parole now, but the years of hardship have embittered him.

One cold, rainy night, Jean Valjean knocks on the door of the saintly Bishop of Digne. Valjean asks only for food scraps, but the bishop invites him inside to eat at the table with him and to spend the night. During the middle of the night, Valjean steals silver from the bishop and then strikes the old man on the face when confronted.

The next day the police capture Valjean and take him back to the bishop's house. Valjean expects to be condemned and sent back to work on a chain gang, perhaps for the rest of his life. But instead the bishop tells the police that the silver was a gift and asks Jean Valjean why he didn't take the most valuable present. He then places silver candlesticks in Valjean's backpack and whispers in his ear, "With this silver I have purchased your soul for God."

When we see Valjean again, eight years have passed. He has a new name, Monsieur Madeleine, and he has become a factory owner and beloved mayor of a small town. The bishop's gift was not squandered. Jean Valjean is a new man, freed from his bitterness and brimming with love. He spends the rest of his life passing on the gift of redemption to others.

Jean Valjean's transformation is in marked contrast to the life of another main character, Javert. The two met when Javert worked as a guard at the prison camp where Valjean was convict number 24601. Javert judges him then as a lawbreaker and refuses to free him from that label.

As fate and Victor Hugo would have it, Javert moves to the same town where Valjean serves as mayor and is named chief of police. In time Javert realizes the identity of Valjean and that he has broken his parole. He dedicates himself to recapturing the convict, and throughout the course of the musical, Javert relentlessly pursues Valjean to return him to prison. Javert is the unrelenting and unforgiving law. Valjean is grace personified.

Nine years pass. The setting has changed to Paris, but Javert's pursuit of

Valjean has not. In a powerful scene, Valjean finds himself in a position to kill Javert and be free of his dogged pursuit. But instead he offers mercy.

Apparently Valjean's dramatic gift of grace shatters the unbending principals of justice on which Javert has based his life. Soon Javert throws himself into the Seine River and dies. The musical continues, but the main point is made. The law is no match for the power of grace.

But there is another point. The bishop changed Valjean's life through the gift of unmerited forgiveness. Valjean's bitterness melted, and his heart became soft and pliable. As a result of receiving forgiveness, he was able to offer forgiveness, and he became a holy conduit through which the love of God was able to flow to others. Forgiveness restored him to life and in the end pushed stone-hearted unforgiveness out of the picture.

An Unnatural Act

Each time I witness an act of forgiveness, I marvel at its power to heal, to break what could have been an unending, transgenerational cycle of pain. Most of us aspire to forgiveness. In a recent Gallup poll, 94 percent of those surveyed nationwide said it was important to forgive. But the same poll suggested that we don't frequently offer forgiveness. Only 48 percent said they usually tried to forgive others. Why?

First of all, forgiveness is unnatural to our lower nature. If we are hit on the face, our instincts don't suggest that we offer a hug or another cheek. It's our nature to seek survival. When we are hurt, either physically or emotionally, we want the person who hurt us to experience our pain. We want to provide him or her with justice, not mercy. And if that person is smaller than we are, we want to administer the sentence ourselves.

But even if we become convinced that it is in our best interest to forgive—that we should listen to our higher nature—we may forgive prematurely or even postmaturely. At times our discomfort in living with bitterness and our guilt over entertaining revengeful images has caused us to blurt out, "I forgive you." But our words were more scheming than sincere. We find it perversely satisfying to identify the person who hurt us as needing our forgiveness. Saying "I forgive you" leaves him or her wearing the label of "sinner" and us wearing the label of "saint." This kind of exchange has nothing to do with forgiveness, with "giving wholly" of myself. At best it is an example of premature forgiveness—saying the right words while anger still rules the heart and blocks the free, in-and-out flow of God's love.

We can also fall into the trap of postmature forgiveness. Sometimes we tell a person, "I forgive you," but only after we have made the person suffer seventy times seven for what he or she had done. We see the offense as giving us permission to release our anger, and we relish being able to hold something over that person's head. Only after we have sufficiently pummeled the offender and decided he or she has had enough, do we say we forgive him or her.

Both scenarios illustrate how we can sometimes go through the motions of forgiveness but miss the heart of forgiveness. Each displays a basic ignorance about how the process really works.

Forgiveness goes against our instincts for survival. We find it extremely difficult to release someone who has hurt us deeply. Fortunately, God exists as a resource who can be tremendously helpful. Let's examine what this means.

THE JOURNEY TOWARD FORGIVENESS

Brad and Kathy met in college. Brad had been a star football player in high school, but he was an inch too short and a quarter of a second too slow to make the college team. So he channeled his competitive energy toward getting into a good law school and dating sorority girls.

Her mother's reflection and her father's pride, Kathy was a high school cheerleader and beauty pageant veteran. For her, success meant being on the receiving end of admiring looks.

I met Brad and Kathy fifteen years after they had graduated from college. They had been married for over fourteen years, and their marriage was falling apart. Neither wanted a divorce, but only because they thought it would devastate their two young children. Neither could stand to be in the same room with the other.

About six months prior, Kathy found out that Brad was having an affair. A divorce law specialist, Brad had gotten involved with one of his clients, and now Kathy was threatening to divorce him. And if it weren't for the children, he wouldn't contest.

For years Brad and Kathy had been growing apart. The truth is, Kathy was a trophy for Brad—a shiny, beautiful object that was impressive to his friends. He didn't really know how to love, nor did he seem to care about who she was on the inside. Brad only knew how to compete and win. From the moment he first saw her, he made it his goal to have Kathy as his own and put her on his shelf.

Kathy was equally insecure. She wanted a white knight to whisk her away from her secret insecurities and treat her like a queen. Brad's apparent self-confidence, outgoing nature, and earning potential made him attractive to her. Plus she didn't mind some parts of being a trophy wife. She liked being admired for her looks.

Over time, however, Kathy began to resent both Brad's control and the attention he devoted to his career. She pulled away from him, hoping he would follow. But he didn't. Instead he tried to force her back with harsh words and insults, and this only drove her further away. The chasm got wider and wider with time, so wide, in fact, that they had given up trying to cross it years before the affair.

But the simmering pot boiled when Kathy discovered a receipt from her favorite jewelry store. The receipt was for some jewelry she had never received. That discovery led to another. Brad's affair had been going on for almost six months.

Kathy's heart, which was already very cold, froze solid. The man she had not liked for years she now hated. The fighting that had been behind closed doors was now erupting in front of their children. Both of them felt trapped and desperate, and they decided to try marriage counseling before calling it quits. That's how they ended up in my office.

As a counselor I often use stories or film clips for insight or subtle motivation, and that's what I did with Brad and Kathy. I wanted to help them understand their natural feelings of hurt and anger and to give them some measure of hope. I also wanted to help them begin to see each other differently, so I told them a fable that Louis Smedes tells in his warm and wise book, *Forgive and Forget.*

Magic Eyes

In the fable, a thin baker named Fouke comes home to find his wife in the act of adultery. The betrayal quickly becomes the talk of the town and the shame of the self-righteous Fouke.

While Fouke announces that he "forgave her as the Good Book said he should," he has not. In actuality he despises her as if she were a common whore, and his judgment allows him to punish her with his righteous mercy.

But he pays a price as well. Each time Fouke feels his secret hate for his wife, an angel drops a small pebble in his heart that weighs him down and causes more pain. He is experiencing a vicious cycle. His hate brings pebbles, pebbles bring pain, and the pain brings more hate. The past cripples him.

But the same angel that has been dropping the pebbles comes and tells Fouke how he can become free. She gives him "magic eyes" that will allow him to empathize with his wife and see her not as the woman who betrayed him but as the weak woman who needed him. Only a new way of seeing can heal the hurt and restore their relationship.

When he protests, "Nothing can change the past," the angel agrees. But she adds, "You cannot change the past, you can only heal the hurt that comes to you from the past. And you can heal it only with the vision of the magic eyes."[1]

Fouke asks for and receives magic eyes. As he begins to see his wife as a needy woman who loves him instead of as a wicked woman who had betrayed him, the angel removes the pebbles one by one.

Smedes' fable in many ways anticipated the forgiveness research of the past decade. Many experts agree that we can move forward in forgiveness when we see the one who has hurt us in a different manner. As we learn to empathize with the one who caused us pain, we enhance our ability to forgive.

After telling them this story, I encouraged Brad and Kathy to ask for a different vision, to learn to see the other as a child in desperate need of love and recognition instead of as a wicked adult. I also encouraged them to be patient with the slow process of having stones removed from a heavy heart.

To help them develop magic eyes, I asked that they watch *Les Misérables* together with a pen and pad of paper. They both were to recall any time in their lives where someone gave them silver candlesticks (unmerited offers of forgiveness) instead of punishment. While neither could remember a significant person who had made such an offer, they both became tearful in discussing how, on more than one occasion, Christ had played the role of the Bishop of Digne in their lives. As they considered how they had each been forgiven, they felt motivated to offer forgiveness to each other.

Two-by-Fours and Forgiveness

I have already referenced two futile ways to attempt forgiveness. Despite their ineffectiveness, many people still use these two approaches—premature and postmature—when trying to forgive someone. In the story about magic eyes, Fouke practiced both. He told his wife, "I forgive you," but it was a premature declaration motivated by his guilt. Subsequently he practiced postmature forgiveness and emitted self-righteous anger.

In order to help Brad and Kathy combat both of these temptations, and to reach out to Jesus for help, I asked them to participate in the following imagery exercise.[2]

"Kathy," I began, "imagine that you walk into a small room with a cement floor and cinder-block walls. High on one of the walls is a small window. Picture Brad sitting on a chair in the center of the room. Ropes bind his legs and arms to the chair, preventing him from leaving the room or even standing up. The only other thing in the room is a two-by-four. It is propped up in the corner of the room.

"See yourself walking over and picking up the board. Feel it in your hands. Then walk over to where Brad is sitting in the chair, and raise the two-by-four over your head to strike him. You are about to bring it down on him, but then you remember that as a Christian you are supposed to forgive him, so you throw the plank away, and say, 'I forgive you. I must.' And then you walk away.

"But your anger still burns within. Your words of forgiveness are premature.

"Imagine next that you are standing over Brad with the board again raised over your head, poised to strike him. Your anger says, *Pay him back… Doesn't the Bible say an eye for an eye?*

"And you say, 'Good idea,' and beat Brad with the piece of wood. You feel great as you release your anger and retaliate for how Brad has hurt you. But the relief quickly passes and things seem even worse. Brad is now angry—and with reason. And he will likely feel that he has the right to strike back.

"Now imagine a third alternative. Imagine standing over Brad with the board raised over your head. As you are standing there, poised to retaliate, you recount the pain you have experienced because of his affair. Allow yourself to experience it again, right here and now. You know that in terms of justice alone, you have the right to hurt him for the pain he has caused you. You feel the pain and say nothing. You do not give in to a premature declaration of forgiveness.

"True forgiveness is not denial or repression, neither is it retaliation. So you resist the temptation to pay him back. You stand ready to strike, feeling the pain, but you do nothing more.

"Now imagine that Jesus enters the room and walks over by your side. You say, 'Jesus, help me. I don't want to pretend that I'm not dying on the inside. But I don't want to make things worse.'"

Then I told her, "Kathy, this is where I have to shut up. I have no idea what your soul most needs to hear. So I'm going to be quiet for a while and allow you to experience whatever Jesus would like to show you or say to you."

And to no one's surprise, Jesus did show up. In her mind's eye, Kathy saw him enter the room and stand by her side. She felt guilty but said to him, "Help me, please. I want to hit him so much, but I know it's the wrong thing to do."

Jesus looked into her eyes, and she felt deeply loved. Slowly her arms came to rest at her sides. Still lost in his gaze, she dropped the two-by-four.

I know you are hurting so badly, she felt Jesus say. *But look at Brad now.*

She looked at where Brad had been sitting, tied to the chair, but what she saw surprised her. She saw an eight-year-old boy holding a football trophy with tears sliding down his cheeks. Somehow she recognized Brad's fear and sensed the deep truth that he was not a monster that wanted to devour, but a little boy who just wanted to be loved and had no idea how to make that happen.

"He's just like me," she sobbed out loud.

Then she felt Jesus say to her, *I want to be with you both. I want to love you and teach you how to love.*

He took her by the hand. But her hand was small. She was a little girl. Together they knelt down by the little boy and untied the ropes.

"Do you want to play with me?" the little boy asked after being untied.

"Yes, we do," she said.

Brad went through this same exercise, and he, too, was able to offer true forgiveness.

SAYING "AS YOU WISH" TO FORGIVENESS

Forgiveness is one of the final passageways to living in love and union with each other and with God. Some people never squeeze through the narrow entrance and live their lives on the outside of the room where union with God is impossible. While Jesus' primary message was the availability of the kingdom of God, we must understand that the kingdom is the realm where the mind, heart, and will of the subjects become one with the mind, heart, and will of the King. Jesus emphasized forgiveness precisely because we cannot live in harmony and union with him if we have unforgiveness in our hearts.

But he also knows that forgiveness is even more difficult to achieve without his help in the process. The best course for us to take is to become willing for him to cut through the ropes that bind us to our anger and then take the two-by-four from our hands, step inside our bodies, and show us how to give wholly so we can again be open to love and union.

~~~~~~

Bible Study: The Parable of the Unmerciful Servant

Text: Matthew 18:21-34

Then Peter came to Jesus and asked, "Lord, how many times shall I forgive my brother when he sins against me? Up to seven times?"

Jesus answered, "I tell you, not seven times, but seventy-seven times.

"Therefore, the kingdom of heaven is like a king who wanted to settle accounts with his servants. As he began the settlement, a man who owed him ten thousand talents was brought to him. Since he was not able to pay, the master ordered that he and his wife and his children and all that he had be sold to repay the debt.

"The servant fell on his knees before him. 'Be patent with me,' he begged, 'and I will pay back everything.' The servant's master took pity on him, canceled the debt and let him go.

"But when that servant went out, he found one of his fellow servants who owed him a hundred denarii. He grabbed him and began to choke him. 'Pay back what you owe me!' he demanded.

"His fellow servant fell to his knees and begged him, 'Be patient with me, and I will pay you back.'

"But he refused. Instead, he went off and had the man thrown into prison until he could pay the debt. When the other servants saw what had happened, they were greatly distressed and went and told their master everything that had happened.

"Then the master called the servant in. 'You wicked servant,' he said, 'I canceled all that debt of yours because you begged me to. Shouldn't you have had mercy on your fellow servant just as I had on you?' In anger his master turned him over to the jailers to be tortured, until he should pay back all he owed."

Observations

This passage begins with Peter's asking Jesus, "Lord, how many times [must] I forgive my brother?" Perhaps the brother Peter has in mind is one of the disciples. Perhaps he is hoping Jesus will say, "Peter, my humble and kind friend, to forgive once is plenty and twice will make you a saint."

But Jesus cares about kingdom living. He uses the question to teach Peter about a radically different way to live, how we are to live. But first he blows the disciple's mind. "How many times should you forgive, Peter? Times without limit."

Then he tells Peter a parable to illustrate both the kingdom and the importance of forgiveness to life in that realm. The king is God. Peter (or any one of us) is the servant whose debts have been forgiven. The fellow servant represents whoever it is that Peter needs to forgive (or anyone we need to forgive).

When we refuse to forgive and instead choose to punish the offender with our words and actions, we take on the role of a righteous king instead of a humble servant. More important, we have devalued what is of supreme value—staying connected by love to God and others.

Reflection Questions

1. How does this parable challenge you to become more willing to offer forgiveness?
2. What is the connection between forgiving others and being able to live in the kingdom of heaven?
3. In what ways have you responded in a similar fashion as the ungrateful servant?
4. What can you do to go back and correct the situation? Commit to do just that.

Meditation: Empathy As Union[3]

Explanation

When we do not forgive the wrongs done to us, we poison our physical, emotional, and spiritual health, sometimes deeply. People have many reasons for holding onto bitterness, ranging from not knowing how to forgive to not wanting to forgive. But if we truly wish to forgive and to be set free from resentment, we can be helped by a willingness to empathize with the one who hurt us, to feel what he or she feels.

Meditation

(*Note:* Do this exercise only if you have had the opportunity to express (at least to yourself) all your resentments. Empathy needs to follow catharsis, or it might lead to denial and premature forgiveness instead of freedom.)

Look back on the entire occasion when someone caused you pain. But this time, consider it from the other person's point of view. In your mind, take his or her place and explain the incident from that perspective. Notice how the incident looks when seen through the eyes of the other. Realize that there is rarely an instance when someone slights, hurts, or attacks you as a result of malice alone. In most instances, it is people who have been deeply wounded themselves who hurt others. Genuinely happy people are not wicked. It may also be helpful to entertain the possibility that you were not *personally* the target of the other's attack. In most cases the offender is attacking something in you that he or she has projected there. It may be that he or she is attacking part of themselves and not you personally. See if all these considerations lead you to feel compassion for the offender rather than anger and resentment alone.

Finally, to strengthen your decision to give up your resentment, do the following.

1. Imagine seeing Jesus on the cross. Picture him in clear detail.
2. Now go back to the scene of your resentment. Stay with it for a while.
3. Return to Jesus crucified and gaze at him again.
4. Keep alternating between the event that caused your resentment and the scene of Jesus on the cross until you notice the resentment slipping away from you and you experience increased feelings of freedom and lightness of heart.
5. Imagine yourself saying, "Father, forgive the person who hurt me. He didn't know what he was doing."

Spiritual Exercise: You and the Two-by-Four

The Setup
This is a very powerful exercise. If you do decide to experience it, it would be wise to try it first with a lesser offender sitting in the chair. It is also an open

exercise. You will be given guidance to a point, but most of what happens will be between you and Jesus. Before beginning, pray for the direction, guidance, and supervision of the Holy Spirit.

The Exercise

Take a few minutes to take yourself through the Five Ps of Prayer. After you have become still and quiet before God, imagine yourself in a small room. At the center of the room, tied to a chair, sits a person who has offended you. In the system of an eye for an eye, you have the right to pay him back. Study the person, using your imagination.

Also in the room is a wooden two-by-four, a club. Pick it up and stand over the person who has offended you. Raise the club over your head, but be careful not to slip into premature forgiveness. Recall how this person hurt you. Replay the memories. Reexperience your pain. Do this until you are aware that you have both the legal right to retaliate and the visceral desire to do so.

Do not strike the person who has hurt you, but do allow your anger to rush out.

At this point you may need some help in finding a way out. Pray that Jesus will step into the room, talk with you, and provide you with the words and images that will lead to true forgiveness. Allow as much time for this as you need.

After completing the exercise, make a mental note of your feelings after following through with what you heard Jesus say. Enjoy any experience of emotional freedom or healing. But resist any temptation to share the experience with anyone who might inform the offender. Forgiveness is for you. It doesn't require participation from the offender. That is the domain of reconciliation.

Chapter 9

Reconciliation

Awakening to the Desire to Be United with God Forever

Holy and gracious Father: In your infinite love you made us for your-self; and when we had fallen into sin and became subject to evil and death, you in your mercy, sent Jesus Christ, your only and eternal son, to share our human nature, to live and die as one of us, to reconcile us to you, then God and Father of all.

BOOK OF COMMON PRAYER

The mystery that has been kept hidden for ages and generations, but is now disclosed to the saints... Christ in you, the hope of glory.

COLOSSIANS 1:26-27

Once upon a time Hank fell in love with a whore. Her name was Gina. Hank knew about Gina's background, but it didn't matter to him. Something about her had captured his heart.

While he didn't know if pleasure, money, or belonging motivated her promiscuity, he didn't really care. He knew all he needed to know—he had fallen for her and was convinced that she loved him too. He asked her to be his wife, and she said yes.

Unfortunately, Gina's past would not stay in the rearview mirror. One day, two months into the marriage, Hank came home from work early and discovered her in the act of infidelity—in their marriage bed.

Hank was angry, but looking at her face, he forgave her in an instant—even as her lover was jumping out the window. It didn't matter to him that she had not said she was sorry for what she had done.

Except for the occasional appearance of tears in his kind eyes, you wouldn't know that Hank was aware of Gina's continued unfaithfulness. Some of his friends tried to convince him he was too naive for his own good, too quick to forgive. But they were the inexperienced ones. They simply didn't know just how deep love can be.

And for Gina, the well of a husband's acceptance had to be very deep. It seemed every visitor to their house, from the UPS man to the cable guy, knew of her need for affection and did his part to fill the void. Her lovers were numerous. She was the talk of the town. Several towns.

In time Hank and Gina had three children. Well, it would be safer to say that Gina had three. Hank wasn't sure if he was the father. But even that didn't matter to him; he loved all of them as if they were his own. He loved them because they were part of Gina.

And that was a good thing for those children, because before the youngest was eating solid food, Gina packed up and left them all crying in the driveway. Hank held the baby as Gina drove away in the passenger seat of a pickup truck, lured by the siren call of a man who promised her gifts and adventure.

Time passed. Gina stayed away from Hank and the children while she searched for excitement—but she received only bruises and heartbreak. Hank did a good job of raising the kids. As far as he was concerned, his marriage to Gina was for better or worse. And it was forever.

Time was not Gina's friend. Her beauty faded. Her hair thinned, her bosom began to sag, and her eyes became dark and hollow. Her handsome lovers no longer wanted her, and she was forced to make her living the only way she knew how, turning ten dollar tricks in backseats and alleys. With a growing drug habit to support, she really needed the money.

Eventually someone told Hank where Gina was living, thinking he would like to know so he could get on with his life and find a woman deserving of his pure love. But the messenger was wrong.

Hank jumped into his car like an excited teenager on a first date. He drove to the city to see his wife. It took two days of searching, but he eventually found her.

He grabbed her and lifted her off the ground with a bear hug. But as he put her back down, she asked him if he wanted a date. Her eyes were dark caves leading to a chemical wasteland. Her distant stare told him that she didn't even recognize him.

Hank picked her back up and gently placed her in the front seat of his car. When her pimp came over and started banging on the hood, Hank got out of the car and gave him a tall stack of hundred-dollar bills. "I'm buying her back for the rest of her life."

He got no further complaints.

Hank drove Gina to a rehab facility close to home and checked her in. He visited three times a day as she became clean and sober. Then he took her back home again. As always, he treated her as if her faithfulness and love were equal to his own.

A Little Story Within a Bigger Story

An amazing tale, wouldn't you say? And yet it's a true story. Perhaps you recognize it. Except for the names, the story is faithful to what actually happened twenty-eight hundred years ago. It's your typical "righteous man falls in love with harlot and refuses to stop loving her no matter what" love story.

Hank's real name was Hosea. Hosea worked as a minor prophet during the middle of the eighth century B.C., and he fell in love with a prostitute named Gomer. But their story is only a dim reflection of one that is much bigger and even more astonishing—the story of God's love for us and the unending lengths to which he will go in pursuit of reconciliation with us.

Up until now our discussion has included things we can do to invite God to change us and live through us. However, we can do nothing to accomplish the mysteries of reconciliation and union with God, which are the next two stages of our journey toward real change. We can do nothing, that is, except to marvel at God's love and open our hearts even wider as we awaken more and more to the excitement, glory, and transformational possibilities of Christ within.

This shift in focus from us to God is not cause for despair, but rejoicing. God would not tease us with an impossible goal. If we will simply whisper, "As you wish," he'll make sure reconciliation and consistent union with him becomes our reality. "He who began a good work in you will carry it on to completion until the day of Christ Jesus" (Philippians 1:6). That's the promise of the story of Hosea and Gomer.

Hosea is also another form of the name Joshua, the name of the man who led Israel into the Promised Land and a name equivalent to the name of the last king of Israel, Hoshea. But more significant, the Greek form of these names is Jesus.

Hosea's life was a parable about the great storyteller, Jesus. It is Jesus to whom this story points like a neon arrow. Jesus is the ultimate picture of faithfulness, love, endurance, compassion, and humility.

Gomer represents the people of Israel. But she also represents the stream of harlots, tax collectors, and sinners that Jesus simply refused to stop loving. These who were so prone to give their love to cheap substitutes are also you and me.

It is the height of unexpected beauty to see love in its purest form...to see an individual of holy character have such love without limits for one who is unholy, immoral, and self-absorbed, and be, after a prolonged separation, willing to joyfully take back the loved one.

In the end, the story of Hosea and Gomer is about reconciliation. It portrays the faithful and boundless love of God. It reveals his invitation to each of us to come back home no matter where we have been or what we have done. No matter how many times we drive off to enjoy adventures with idols, Jesus pursues us to the edge of insanity and offers us a ride back home. There are no limits to the lengths to which God will go to awaken our desire to be with him forever.

First, Middle, and Last

Because we were designed to live in love, we can't experience abundant living apart from reconciliation. The process of our reconciliation with God is a journey from antagonism to friendship, from enmity to union.

One of the most striking differences between ancient Christianity, which was Eastern, and much of its modern Western counterpart is the contrast between their respective views of reconciliation. While admittedly an oversimplification, today's Protestant church has generally defined reconciliation with God, or salvation, in legal, judicial, or forensic terms.[1] Christ's death pays the just penalty for our sin, and we become reconciled to God by virtue of our faith in his meritorious sacrifice. While not denying the sacrificial aspect of reconciliation, earlier church traditions view reconciliation as a journey of transformation and the fulfillment of the image of God in humankind.

Reconciliation is comprised of the first, middle, and last steps of the journey back to union with God. The more we are willing to lay aside our desire for self-rule, the more *with* and *like* Christ we become.

James L. Fowle, pastor of Chattanooga's First Presbyterian Church from 1929 to 1967 and president of Chattanooga Bible Institute for more than four decades, viewed reconciliation as a journey as well. One afternoon a zealous sidewalk evangelist, not knowing the identity of his target, raced up to Dr. Fowle, thrust a tract in his face and asked, "Are you saved?"

Dr. Fowle replied: "Yes, I *was* saved from the penalty of sin by the sacrificial death of the Lord Jesus Christ. I *am being* saved from the power of sin by the indwelling of the Holy Spirit in my life. And I *will be saved* from the presence of sin when I meet God the Father face to face in heaven."

I tell this story because I don't want our focus on reconciliation to be confusing. Christ's birth, life, death, and resurrection accomplished reconciliation between God and humankind. When we accept this amazing gift, it's the beginning point of salvation and our journey as Christians into Christlikeness. But reconciliation is not simply a one-time event. It also has a progressive aspect. It's a romantic and continuing journey of conversation, communion, and union with God during which we learn to lay aside the idols that separate us from him. It's a continuing adventure in coming together with God.

As the old sermon illustration goes, a broken ship is safe when it is towed into a harbor. But it is still broken and incapable of a successful voyage unless it is repaired and made new. The journey of transformation is the process of reconciliation during which our hearts become completely renovated and seaworthy.

The Incarnation As Reconciliation

If the story of Hosea and Gomer stretches the heart, how can our chests contain the account of Jesus? The difference between Jesus and you and me defies imagination. Jesus was more superior to humanity than a king is to a mud-encrusted pig. Yet he emptied himself of all his privileges and leaped inside our pigpen. The King of glory traveled across light-years of space to the very edge of his divinity to pick us up, gaze into our hollow eyes, and take us back home.

Several years ago I scribbled the following poem while reflecting on the love displayed in Jesus' willingness to become incarnate (literally, the *in-flesh-*

ment of God) and on what that must have meant for him.² Consider these words as you imagine Jesus becoming incarnate, just for you.

Incarnation

All-Powerful God—helpless in a manger
Omniscient Mind—confined between the ears of a toddler
Eternal God—confined in time
Omnipresent King—traveling by foot
Creator of the Universe—swinging a hammer
Source of Living Water—parched in the wilderness
Lion of Judah—Lamb of God
Author of Truth—accused by liars
Prince of Peace—beaten by soldiers
The Word of God—edited
The Author of Life—dead in a tomb
Light of the World—shining again from a once-dark tomb
All-Powerful God—becoming like me for a time
So that I could be like him forever

While the story of the prodigal son is a powerful picture of God's love, in the incarnation we see a lover who doesn't stop at the end of the driveway and wait. No, the Lover of our souls cannot wait for our return. He runs across the countryside and steps into the mud and muck where we sit. He invades our shame and refuses to let us hide from his loving face.

In the words of fourteenth-century monk Nicolas Cabasilas:

It was He who came to the earth and retrieved his own image, and He came to that place where the sheep was straying and He lifted it up and stopped it from straying. He did not remove us from here, but He made us heavenly while yet remaining on earth, and imparted to us the heavenly life without leading us up to heaven, but by bending heaven to us and bringing it down. As the prophet says, "he bowed the heavens also, and came down" (Ps. 18:9).

Christ humbled himself and became one of us to invite us back home to live as princes and princesses in his kingdom. But he did even more than become like us and live among us. He showed us how to live—in obedience to the Father, regardless of the cross. Jesus accepted a horrific form of death and offered us all the riches he possessed. Then he rose from the dead and proved he had the right to make such an offer.

THE RESURRECTION AS RECONCILIATION

I have a friend whom few people can stand to be around. He's a militant atheist, which doesn't play well in the barbershops and restaurants of our small, Bible Belt town.

Tom claims to have read more than three thousand books on religion and theology. And if you listen to him talk, you don't doubt the number—just the wisdom of some of his selections. Tom has also taken every class the philosophy and religion departments of a major state university have to offer.

Tom and I have an informal reading club. Several months back I agreed to read some of what he considers the most challenging books to the Christian faith. Tom, on the other hand, agreed to read folks like C. S. Lewis and George MacDonald. Then we discuss what we've read.

I like having an atheist for a friend. For one thing, it forces me to take all the clichés out of my vocabulary. We've had some interesting dialogues.

But there is one question I've posed to Tom that he refuses to answer. Every time I place it on the table, he immediately clears his throat and tries to cover it with off-topic footnotes from his latest reading. Here's the question:

If Jesus came to earth and spent three years hanging out with a band of twelve followers, and each proved himself to be a sniveling coward at the time of Jesus' arrest and crucifixion, what could possibly have happened that turned them into superheroes just weeks after Jesus was dead and buried? Certainly not the rotting body of a madman.

I can think of only one possible answer to that question. It's the actuality of the resurrection of Jesus from the dead and his appearance before his friends. Through his incarnation, Jesus demonstrated his unfathomable love. Through his death, he demonstrated radical surrender to his Father's will and his desire for reconciliation. Through his resurrection, Jesus demonstrated that he was who he said he was—the Son of God—and that he had the power to undo the damage of Eden.

THE RECONCILING POWER OF THE RISEN CHRIST

Picture the scene. The disciples are gathered in the Upper Room where they have retreated in fear and confusion after Jesus was crucified. They are hiding out as a group, collectively shaking, the same way Adam and Eve did after the Fall.

And just as Adam and Eve chose to grasp and hide instead of to trust and approach, so have the disciples, Jesus' closest friends. At the crucial moment, they reached out and clutched after their safety. Now they are hiding. Their shame must have been palpable.

Then, despite the locked doors, Jesus stands in their midst, a light in their darkness. And there are his disciples, who symbolize us all after we have made the wrong choices. Adam with his apple, Gomer with her lover, all of us gripping the scripts of the future we are writing for ourselves. There we all are: frightened, alone, drowning in the shame of self-rule, in the embrace of false love.

But the risen Christ breaks through the walls. He has gone to the darkest places and returned for us. He wastes no time, immediately offering simple and direct comfort.

"Peace be with you."

Peace. Shalom. The tranquil and fear-free state of existence partially actualized in Eden. The deepest longing of every human heart, the very air of the kingdom.

Peace. The serenity that can only come when we abandon all separation from God. Forever-connectedness with Christ and full participation in the life and love of God. True reconciliation brings shalom. To be within the intimacy of the Father and Son is what it means to live in shalom.

Imagine what the disciples must have been thinking. *We cursed your name and denied we even knew you, and you still love us. We abandoned you to murderers who beat you and tortured you beyond belief, and you have come back to us with presents. We have tried to distance ourselves from you and have locked you out, yet you walk through the door in order to bring us back home. We admit that we can never live the life you have in mind for us, and you say, "No problem. I will live it through you."*

As we reflect and meditate on the lengths God will go to offer us reconciliation and to provide us with the strength to live life in a whole new way, we find the will to let go of self-rule and freedom from the shame that pushed us into hiding. In defeating death, Christ proved all his promises can come true. He can make us more like him.

VESSELS OF INCARNATION

Because Jesus was able to free himself from the grip of death, it became possible for him to be incarnate again, countless times, in the flesh of folks like you and me. As we surrender more and more of ourselves to his indwelling presence, we move toward union and become more and more like him. In surrender we become vessels of incarnation.

I have a friend who refers to this process as slowly being taken over by an alien, which isn't a bad description. He tells the following story.

One evening after a hard day of work, he is sitting on the couch watching SportsCenter. He isn't thinking about being like Jesus. The only thing he wants to imitate is a potato.

But from his perch he can see the pile of dirty dishes that clutters the kitchen counter, and he realizes his wife will be home soon. And then he hears it, a gentle whisper: *Let's go wash the dishes. It'll make Susan so happy to walk in and see a clean kitchen.*

Since he is the only person home, there is no mistaking the target of the communication. So almost without thinking he gets up off the couch and walks into the kitchen to scrub pots and wash dishes, talking to God all the while.

His wife returns as he's rinsing suds from the last pot. She beams a smile at him. He just shrugs his shoulders and says, "It's that alien again."

A man in a small house in the suburbs of Atlanta is learning to surrender to love. And that night he experiences how reconciliation can lead to union—spiritual and otherwise.

THE LOVER WHO WON'T STOP HIS PURSUIT

The story of God is about reconciliation, pure and simple. The Lover of our soul will not stop his pursuit, no matter what we have done or where we have been.

Even after a thirty-three-year absence from home, Jesus would not return to the joy of heaven until he had reconciled with a fallen friend.

Jesus' appearance before his band of followers was only one of many after his resurrection. Before he returned home, he revealed his love to more than five hundred people. One of the most poignant of these scenes occurred on the shores of the Sea of Galilee.

In the twenty-first chapter of John's gospel, we find another wonderful example of Christ's invitation to reconciliation and a relationship of intimate love.

Jesus is down to his last few hours before making a final ascent into heaven. But he cannot leave without a face-to-face reconciliation with one he loved so dearly: the rugged, pigheaded Peter.

Jesus orchestrates a scene that reminds Peter of his initial call into ministry—fishing again with his friends on the Sea of Galilee.[3]

As they labor, catching nothing all night, Jesus is preparing breakfast for them on the beach. The meal is almost ready. Jesus shouts to tell them where to locate 153 fish and then invites them to come and have breakfast. At the sound of Jesus' voice, Peter swims in the water like an Olympic athlete. So desperate is he to be with Jesus that he races the boat to shore.

When the disciples finish eating, Jesus calls Peter aside and asks him, three times, if he truly loves him—once for each of Peter's rejections forty-three days before.

Jesus says, "Simon, son of John, do you truly love me?"

"Truly love" refers to an adoration that involves the entire personality, including the will. It's a love that races up to romantic love and then blows past. It is a love of union—total unity of personality, including the will, with Jesus.

Peter replies that he "loves" Jesus. But the word he uses simply implies a brotherly love or fondness.

If your spouse asked you if you were head over heels, wholeheartedly in love with him or her, so much that you have no will apart from his or her own, would you dare to reply, "Yes, dear. You know I'm fond of you"?

No, of course not!

And Jesus, as part of the restoration of Peter and his invitation to restored relationship, wants him to feel the difference between these two types of love.

Maybe Peter was still feeling sheepish after his bitterly painful denial of Christ. Maybe he can hardly imagine that Jesus is inviting him to a deep love relationship.

But that is Jesus' invitation to Peter, and he has been asking the same question for almost two thousand years. He's asking you and me right now.

"Are you head over heels in love with me? Will you live your life so close to me that our wills are united and our hearts beat as one?"

How can we help but say, "Yes, Jesus, I want to truly love you, to be one with you. Please keep talking with me until I learn how to move from 'fondness' to union! And thanks for the breakfast!"

THE SHALOM OF EDEN REDUX

This chapter has been an attempt to describe the clean and powerful energy of spiritual fusion—reconciliation—and to underscore how far God will go to offer it to you.

To become reconciled with another means that a former state of friendship, once broken, is now restored. The broken pieces of an ideal are put back together. What was two is now one. Harmonious relationship is now the enjoyed reality.

In reconciliation with God, we once again experience the shalom of Eden as we walk with God as our foreparents did in naked vulnerability.

Bible Study: The Ministry of Reconciliation

Text: Ephesians 2:12-18; 2 Corinthians 5:16-21

Remember that at that time you were separate from Christ, excluded from citizenship in Israel and foreigners to the covenants of the promise, without hope and without God in the world. But now in Christ Jesus you who once were far away have been brought near through the blood of Christ.

For he himself is our peace, who has made the two one and has destroyed the barrier, the dividing wall of hostility, by abolishing in his flesh the law with its commandments and regulations. His purpose was to create in himself one new man out of the two, thus making peace, and in this one body to reconcile both of them to God through the cross, by which he put to death their hostility. He came and preached peace to you who were far away and peace to those who were near. For through him we both have access to the Father by one Spirit.

So from now on we regard no one from a worldly point of view. Though we once regarded Christ in this way, we do so no longer. Therefore, if anyone is in Christ, he is a new creation; the old has gone, the new has come! All this is from God, who reconciled us to himself through Christ and gave us the ministry of reconciliation: that God was reconciling the world to himself in Christ, not counting men's sins against them. And he has committed to us the message of reconciliation. We are therefore Christ's ambassadors, as though God were making his appeal through us. We implore you on Christ's behalf: Be reconciled to God. God made him who had no sin to be sin for us, so that in him we might become the righteousness of God.

Observations

The greatest impact of the Fall—Adam and Eve's pursuit of autonomy—was the loss of relationship with God. Scripture from that point forward tells two stories. One is the story of Gomer and the tens of thousands like her who continually pursue false love. The other story is that of Hosea (or Jesus) and his pursuit of us.

The story of division and reconciliation also happens inside every human being. Internally we are faced with a battle between the false self and the true self. Jesus is so desperate for this battle to end well that he becomes incarnate, submits to death on a cross, and finally becomes willing to step inside the believer to live his life through us.

The lengths God will go for reconciliation seem limitless. So are the benefits of accepting his offer.

Reflection Questions

1. How would you describe the reconciling work of God—both between and within individuals?
2. What does it mean to you to be charged with the ministry of reconciliation?

Meditation: Reconciliation and Acceptance

Explanation

If you have found it helpful to do so, you may want to begin this meditation with the Five Ps of Prayer. After quieting yourself, carefully consider the following questions. After a slow examination of each, offer a prayer for God to assist you in moving toward reconciliation.

Meditation

1. Reconciliation with God
   a. What attitudes in my life cause me to be alienated from God?
   b. Where am I angry and displeased with the way God is handling my affairs?
   c. Do I really believe the teaching found in Romans 8:28: "God works for the good of those who love him"?

    d. What is the status of my daily relationship with God as a friend and lover?

2. Reconciliation with Other Individuals

    a. From whom do I feel somewhat alienated at present?

    b. Which relationship should I start working on first?

    c. What can I do to become reconciled with these persons?

    d. What changes can I make in my attitude to make it easier for others to become reconciled to me?

3. Reconciliation with Community

    a. Where do I feel alienated from various groups to which I belong (for example, family, relatives, peer group, church, work environment)?

    b. What can I do to become more reconciled to or accepting of each of these communities?

    c. How can I bring about better community understanding?

    d. Where should I begin?

4. Reconciliation with Yourself

    a. Who usually wins the battle between my true and false selves?

    b. What can I do to affect this outcome?

    c. Am I my own best friend? How so?

    d. In what ways do I need to forgive myself for past mistakes?

Spiritual Exercise: The Reconciliation of a Penitent

Explanation

It has often been said that the birth of modern psychotherapy is due in part to the loss of the confession in much of Western Christianity. What follows is a simple exercise in confession found in the *Book of Common Prayer*. If you are not part of a church body that offers the practice of confession, take some time during your private devotions to do this confession exercise. Envision Jesus as your priest and imagine him saying the words to be spoken by a priest. Fill in the words of confession as you feel moved by the Holy Spirit.

Exercise

The penitent begins: Bless me, for I have sinned.

The priest says: The Lord be in your heart and upon your lips that you may truly and humbly confess your sins: In the Name of the Father and of the Son and of the Holy Spirit. Amen.

The penitent says: I confess to almighty God, to his church, and to you that I have sinned by my own fault in thought, word, and deed, in things done and left undone; especially ———. For these and all other sins which I cannot now remember, I am truly sorry. I pray God to have mercy on me. I firmly intend amendment of life, and I humbly beg forgiveness of God and his church and ask you for counsel, direction, and absolution.

The priest may at this point offer counsel, direction, and comfort.

The priest makes the Pronouncement of Absolution: Our Lord Jesus Christ, who offered himself to be sacrificed for us to the Father and who conferred power on his church to forgive sins, absolve you through my ministry by the grace of the Holy Spirit and restore you in the perfect peace of the church. Amen.

The priest adds: The Lord has put away all your sins.

The penitent responds: Thanks be to God.

The priest concludes: Go (or abide) in peace and pray for me, a sinner.

Chapter 10

Union with God

Less of Me, More of Him

*With all the will of my heart I assented to be wholly God's.... Sud-
denly the Trinity filled my heart full of the greatest joy, and I understood that it will feel like that in heaven.... The Trinity is our
everlasting lover, the Trinity is our endless joy and bliss, by our Lord
Jesus Christ and in our Lord Jesus Christ.*

JULIAN OF NORWICH

*The kingdom of heaven is like a king who prepared a wedding ban-
quet for his son.*

MATTHEW 22:2

In the film *Tuck Everlasting*, a kaleidoscope of images appears that seem lifted
from the album of Christian spirituality. One poignant scene reminds me of
our dance toward intimacy with God.

Jesse Tuck is one of the two central characters. He and his family have a
great secret: They will live forever. Each has drunk from a mysterious spring
that provides eternal life. Jesse has been seventeen for more than one hundred
years.

But he has a problem. He has fallen in love with a mortal named Winnie
and wants her to join him for the next few thousand years.

One afternoon Jesse and Winnie are exploring in the woods. They come to a large swimming hole, and Jesses dives in and calls for Winnie to join him.

But Winnie says she's too afraid. After Jesse's unsuccessful attempts at coaxing, she finally confesses that she cannot swim. But he is insistent and assures her that he will not let her drown.

Winnie musters her courage and jumps in. Immediately she begins flailing in fear, calling Jesse's name. He comes up behind her, gently lifts her body into a floating position, and says, "Relax against me."

After a while he asks, "Do you like the feeling?"

She answers, "I love it. It feels wonderful. I'm weightless."

"We're carrying you," he says. "You see? The water and me—we're carrying you."

"Don't ever let me go," Winnie tells him.

"There's no chance of that Winnie Foster. I'm never gonna let you go."

In many ways this scene illustrates the process of developing a romantic relationship with God. God offers us the gift of everlasting life and calls us to himself, into a place of risk and bliss, a place we have no ability or inclination to enter on our own. But when we borrow his faith and dive in, he comes to our aid and holds us up. We feel weightless and at peace, lost in the moment, buoyed by grace. In the water of life we rest and experience union with the One we love. Time stands still. We feel connected to everything that is good. And we hear God's reassuring words, "I will never leave you nor forsake you."

Many of us have had brief times of harmony with Jesus. Moments of joy, glimpses of eternity. Such encounters are not unusual. What is unusual, however, is the choice to stay in the water. The film's bittersweet ending is a sobering reminder of this. Winnie chooses not to drink from the fountain of life. Even after having experienced a foretaste of union with God, many of us find it difficult to stay on a course that leads to union with God for more and more moments each day.

Still, the goal of Christian living, both present and future, is union with

God. The signposts appear everywhere in Scripture. Let's look at four of them, each one a picture of the spiritual union to which we are called.

MARRIAGE: UNION BETWEEN A MAN AND WOMAN

From the backdrop of a wedding feast for Jesus' first miracle to his return as a groom eager to greet his bride, the biblical writers used marriage as a prominent metaphor for our relationship with God. Why? Because central to both is a journey toward union and the production of new life.

To more fully appreciate the symbolism of marriage and to better understand how we should live as we await our Groom's return, it helps to know a little about Jewish marriage customs at the time of Jesus.

During Jesus' time, Jewish parents chose who their children would marry. (As the father of two daughters, I like that.) A couple's formal engagement period was kicked off when the bride gave her consent to her parents' choice of her husband. After the bride's first "I do," both families formally sealed a covenant, and the bride and groom became legally bound together, though not yet married.

When that happened, the betrothed groom would immediately begin to work on the bridal chamber, which involved adding a room to his father's house. This was where the couple would honeymoon for seven days—or more—during the marriage festival. The groom's father would inspect the room to decide whether it was suitable and to declare when the groom and bride could enter the chamber.

The law required that the groom, or his father, come up with a price for the bride—usually a large sum of money. (My wife and I are considering telling our daughters that we are reinstating this tradition.) Some grooms had to do hard labor for years to raise the required sum. Just ask Jacob. The bride price symbolized the exchange of the groom's life for the life of the bride[1] and echoed the blood covenant in Jewish tradition. It also created a strong bond between the two families.[2]

Meanwhile, the bride would spend her time preparing for and anticipating her wedding. She would undergo a process of purification that included ritual baths to ensure both cleanliness and virginity. She would also wear a veil as a symbol of separation from others and commitment to her husband.

As part of the anticipation, she lived with a sense of "When will my beloved come for me?" Every night before going to bed, she would prepare an oil lamp in case her groom returned for her after dark. Night after night she would listen for the sound of a shofar, the ram's horn that would precede the arrival of the groom's wedding party.

On the day of the wedding, the bridegroom would go to the bride's house, accompanied by friends, musicians, and singers. The bride would dress in white and wear all the jewels her family could afford. Her parents would present her to the groom with their blessing.

The groom would then lead the wedding party back to his house—that's right, back then the groom's family paid for the reception. Along the way other friends of the couple would join the party. And it would be some party. The feasting would last for one or even two weeks, and the festivities would include music, joking, nightly trips to the nuptial chamber, and the anticipation of new life.

Against this backdrop, the wedding imagery in Scripture becomes even more meaningful. Each aspect of the Jewish ceremony has a symbolic parallel in the wedding of Christ to his bride.

When we became Christians, a covenant of commitment was formed between us, the bride, and Jesus, the Groom. He and his Father have already paid a very high price for us. The Groom literally exchanged his life for ours. And now he and the Father are preparing an addition to their house. No expense is being spared in anticipation of the day we will arrive.

Meanwhile, we are to be in a time of purification and anticipation, each night going to bed in excited expectation about the festivities that await us. Each day we participate in a process of being cleansed and transformed, awash with the Word and energy of Christ.

Unlike the Jewish tradition, however, the consummation of this relationship is not put off until some future date. As Christians we are already the bride of Christ. We have made vows of commitment and have entered into a covenant relationship. We are already united with him.[3]

In a healthy marriage and in a healthy relationship with God:

- *The level of communication is both lovable and intimate.* In an ideal marriage, communication, be it with words or silence, flows from loving hearts. Listen to how Frank Laubach described his communication with God in a strikingly romantic fashion: "It is my business to look into the very face of God until I ache with bliss.... Now I like the Lord's presence so much that when for a half hour or so He slips out of mind—as He does many times a day—I feel as though I had deserted Him, and as though I had lost something very precious in my life."[4]

- *Communication is not a chore but an overflow of joy.* In a healthy marriage, spouses do not view communication as a task that must be checked off, like washing dishes or balancing the checkbook. It happens naturally as a by-product of the relationship. It is another way of touching and being touched, knowing and being known.

- *The communication is ongoing.* While intimate mates feel no obligation to talk to fill silence, their communication is an unending series of sentences, paragraphs, and chapters. The book never ends and is never forgotten on the nightstand. Additionally, communication is not simply for the purpose of asking something of the other, such as: "Will you please iron my shirt?" It is about opening the window to one's soul, not for placing an order.

- *The communication leads to communion.* In a healthy marriage, conversation ascends to the height of communion, a place of more intimate sharing and deep rapport.

- *Communion leads to consummation, ecstasy, and new life.* When a married couple experiences communion (connection, intimacy, and deep sharing) in their relationship, physical intimacy and union typically follow. The joy of emotional union is the best form of foreplay to physical union.

In a happy marriage—be it between people or between an individual and God—love moves toward consummation the way a Jewish groom marched to his bride's house: with great excitement and expectancy. In the act of union, the couple's bodies connect and experience the profound sense of emotional and spiritual oneness. As a result of this union, new life can be created, and through that product of love, even more affection can be experienced.

Marriage and sexual union paint us a picture of the permanent intimacy of our relationship with God. But as good as this analogy is, it's not the best. The Trinity is our best picture of the type of union we are to experience with God.

THE TRINITY: UNION WITHIN GOD

Just twenty-six verses into the Bible, God reveals to us that he is a community: "Then God said, 'Let *us* make man in *our* image'" (Genesis 1:26, emphasis added). And in the initial act of the incarnation, we again see the Trinity. God the Father sends God the Holy Spirit upon Mary, and she conceives Jesus, who is God the Son (see Luke 1:35).

When Jesus got baptized, the witnesses heard God's voice from heaven as he gushed about his Son, saying, "This is my beloved Son, in whom I am well pleased." (Matthew 3:17, KJV). At that same moment the Holy Spirit could not contain himself either. He glides to earth in the form of a dove, descending from the Father and resting upon the shoulder of the Son. Here again we catch a glimpse of the unity that is God.

At God's essence we find unity and communion. Tradition and Scripture teach us that the Trinity is not a thing or abstraction. The Trinity is a community whose members draw their identities from each other. But why? Why does God exist in community? There is only one reason. Love. God is love. And God would not be love unless he could exist in a society of mutual compassion and submission. Love needs others.

The Trinity is the most powerful metaphor in the universe for how a Christian is to live: creatively, compassionately, and in community—united in purpose, separate as individuals, aflame with the energy of divine love. God exists as we are to exist: in harmonious union with him.

This is the only life that will make us happy. While we are not invited to turn the Trinity into a gospel quartet, we are invited to sing along, to join the group, and unite in harmony. We are invited to intimate connection with the three-in-one God.

Now for the third picture of union: the branch and the vine.

THE BRANCH AND THE VINE: UNION BETWEEN GOD AND PEOPLE

From Scripture we also learn that through the mystery of the Trinity, God is *within* us (Spirit), *with* us (Son), and *above and beyond* us (Father). And it gets even better, more intimate. Jesus says that he and his Father are one, and then adds that he wants us to be one with him too.[5]

Listen to the words of Jesus:

I am the vine; you are the branches. If a man remains in me and I in him, he will bear much fruit; apart from me you can do nothing. (John 15:5)

As the Father has loved me, so have I loved you. Now remain in my love. (John 15:9)

I pray…that all of them may be one, Father, just as you are in me and I am in you. May they also be in us so that the world may believe that you have sent me. (John 17:20-21)

God wants us to be as close to him as a branch is to a vine. Connected. United. One an extension of the other. With a vine and branch, it is not possible to tell where one starts and the other ends. It is to be the same with God and us. Just as the branch constantly draws nutrition from the vine, we are to draw our life from God. The same life that is in the branch is to be in us. This both exhilarates and frightens as separation from union means certain death for the branch.

No doubt you've experienced wisps of feeling that connected to God. Perhaps it happened to you in church, while walking through the woods, or while watching the sun as it set over rolling ocean waves. For a moment time seemed to stand still. The awareness of each of your six senses seemed to peak as you suddenly felt swept up into the current of life, lost in a frozen moment. Distractions and anxieties were swept away. The world seemed perfect, and you felt alive in God, dissolved into pure love. You were a branch; God was the vine. Those words came alive.

Such encounters of connection can revolutionize a person's life. Unitive experiences have made drunks sober and caused hard-nosed academics—like C. S. Lewis—to be surprised and forever changed by the experience of pure joy. Such experiences bring to life Jesus' invitation to be organically connected to God and cause us to move increasingly toward consistent union.

COMMUNITY: UNION AMONG PEOPLE

The early church was a radical community of love. They were united, of one heart and soul, married to God, aflame with Trinitarian love, connected to their "Daddy" and to each other like branches into a vine. The early church was a magnificent living organism. The world marveled at its vitality and wanted in.

Listen to Luke's description:

The whole congregation of believers was united as one—one heart, one mind! They didn't even claim ownership of their own possessions. No one said, "That's mine; you can't have it." They shared everything. The apostles gave powerful witness to the resurrection of the Master Jesus, and grace was on all of them.

And so it turned out that not a person among them was needy. Those who owned fields or houses sold them and brought the price of the sale to the apostles and made an offering of it. The apostles then distributed it according to each person's need.

Joseph, called by the apostles "Barnabas" (which means "Son of Comfort"), a Levite born in Cyprus, sold a field that he owned, brought the money and made an offering of it to the apostles. (Acts 4:32-37, MSG)

Why were people attracted to the early church? Because it gave them a visible and functioning example of the kingdom life Jesus had announced. The early church was a community united by the love of God.

Community, the union of people with people, is the fourth great symbol of unity found in Scripture. But unless it has its roots embedded in the water of life and soil of the kingdom, it will begin to wither and die.

In the words of C. S. Lewis: "When Christians speak of being 'in Christ' or of Christ being 'in them'…they mean that Christ is actually operating through them; that the whole mass of Christians are the physical organism through which Christ acts—that they are the cells of His body."[6]

Scripture is a gallery crammed with portraits of union with God. These images are not to remain dusty tributes to a life by and by. The desire for union with God can be a consuming fire burning within the hearts of all Christians. Consistent unity with God can be our here-and-now reality.

BECOMING A CHILD OF LIGHT

As we journey toward consistent union with God, we take on more and more of the character of Christ. In the language of the apostle Paul this means becoming "children of light."[7] The following encounter between a pupil and a spiritual director helps to clarify what this phrase means.

> Abba Lot went to see Abba Joseph and said to him, "Abba, as far as
> I can I say my little office, I fast a little, I pray and meditate, I live in
> peace and as far as I can, I purify my thoughts. What else can I do?"
> Then the old man stood up and stretched his hands towards heaven.
> His fingers became like ten lamps of fire and he said to him, "If you
> will, you can become all flame."[8]

In union, the final stage of spiritual formation, our hearts become aflame with the power and presence of Christ. While this stage will not reach full fruition until we get to heaven, we can achieve overall harmony between God and ourselves on this side of our eulogies. We can experience complete surrender to the presence and will of God. We can experience union *with* God and *within* our own beings.

In *Renovation of the Heart,* Dallas Willard discusses how this happens. His model of transformation is simple and practical but simultaneously profound and comprehensive. He proposes that each of us has these six basic aspects or components.

1. *Thought* (images, concepts, judgments, inferences)
2. *Feeling* (sensations, emotions)

3. *Choice* (will, heart, spirit, decision, character, your "CEO")
4. *Body* (action, interaction with the physical world)
5. *Social Context* (personal and structural relations to others)
6. *Soul* (integrates all of the above to form one life)

WILLARD'S MODEL OF THE PERSON

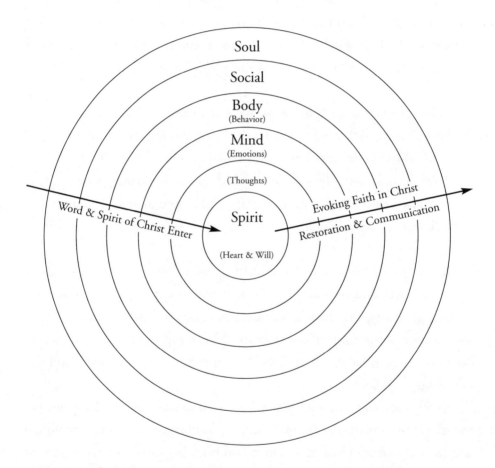

In this figure[9] the first five components correspond to the only five things we can do: think, feel, choose (will), behave, and interact with others. The sixth element—the soul—is the invisible computer that keeps everything running and integrated into one person.

Notice the arrow coming in from the left. This illustrates how the word and spirit of Christ can penetrate to the center of our being. The practice of spiritual disciplines—the little things we can do by direct effort, the "crumbs and bubbles" of formation—enhance our ability to recognize, enjoy, and surrender to the presence of Christ. Brokenness and receptivity bring about real change. Transformation happens as we become open to a real and renovating relationship with Christ. It happens as we become progressively dissatisfied with our ability to manage our life and become more open to God's rule.

Notice also the arrow to the right. Through interacting with Christ and evoking faith in him, we reestablish a relationship with God in which all the aspects of our "self" (thoughts, emotions, will, behavior, social interactions) enter into the process of transformation—into fuller likeness to Christ. Through entering into a relationship with God of progressive intimacy and surrender, we experience real change in every area of our person. Through trust we invite Christ into the center of our being; through faith we allow him to transform all of our innermost parts.

Through the mystery of Christ within, I become less of me and more of him—more and more like Jesus until union with God is the reality of my own personal experience. As this process reaches fruition, we begin to say with the apostle Paul, "To live is Christ and to die is gain" (Philippians 1:21). We become united with Christ through loving surrender. Real change happens one small "As you wish" at a time.

Through progressive surrender and union we can become children of light. Our thoughts can turn constantly to God. Love can become our dominant emotion. Our will can turn soft and pliable in obedience to God. Without thinking, our body can do what is right and good. We can relate to others with transparency and love.[10] We can be aflame with the presence of God.

ONE UNITED SOUL

My father became a child of light. He came into this world behind in the count. He was one of fifteen children born to sharecropper parents. By the time he was ten years old, he could pick two hundred pounds of cotton a day. For his family, the school year played second fiddle to the crops. But poverty and hard labor were the least of his problems. My father was born with bad wiring in his brain: schizophrenia.

By all rights Dad should have ended up in an institution. But he didn't. Instead, when he was a teenager he fell deeply in love with God and lived his life monastically devoted to God. Each day he enjoyed a simple rhythm of work, prayer, and Scripture reading. He wore out a dozen Bibles, and the knees of his pants almost always seemed worn. His mind and his conversations were filled with his love for God.

My dad lived his life unplugged from the "real" world of nickels, noses, and nightly news; he lived his life plugged into the kingdom. And it worked. He was the only one in his family to attend college. He graduated as the valedictorian of his class, married a loving wife, and pastored churches like Francis of Assisi might have done for more than fifty years. He even appeared on national television as a *700 Club* testimony of the year.

Given his early disadvantages, you might expect that my father would have died in an institution or a homeless shelter. But that wasn't the case. The church was packed for his funeral with people whose lives he had touched for God. Some knew the whole story, some didn't. But almost everyone who shook my hand said the same things: "Your father loved God more than anybody I ever knew. That man lived to pray. Your Dad was more like Jesus than anyone I ever met. I think he visited people in the hospital every day."

My father was from another world. He was one of the few full-time residents of the kingdom of heaven who lived and breathed among us, a Protestant saint on loan to earth. He lived each moment of every day in harmonious union with God. Whenever he mentioned Jesus, the smile on his face broadened and became so bright you didn't notice anything else.

My father is my inspiration to a life of union with God. I've read about the saints, but I've also lived with one. I wish I had told him face-to-face what I just typed. But he's home now—where I'm sure he fits like a hand in a glove. But except for actually being able to see God now, I doubt he notices much difference.

It's Better Than Sex

Throughout the centuries the devotion masters have described the experience of surrender to the love of God in sexual terms, using words such as *ecstasy*, being *ravished* by God, *merging* with God, and *union*. And such language must be used. Sexual intimacy is a metaphor for the ultimate spiritual experience, not the other way around.

Why is spiritual union better than physical union? Spiritual union is more holistic than sex; it produces a unity across each component of the person, and the by-product of joy lasts longer than with the physical counterpart. Plus, age does not affect the working parts, and there is no temptation to smoke afterward!

We are designed to live connected to each other and to God. As Larry Crabb so beautifully describes the soul-healing power of connection:

> When two people *connect*, when their beings intersect as closely as two
> bodies during intercourse, something is poured out of one and into the
> other that has power to heal the soul of its deepest wounds and restore
> it to health. The one who receives experiences the joy of being healed.
> The one who gives knows the even greater joy of being used to heal.
> Something good is in the heart of each of God's children that is more
> powerful than everything bad. It's there, waiting to be released, to work
> its magic.[11]

Union with God results from falling head over heels in love with him, so much so that we become willing for our heart to become a manger for his presence. And like union with a spouse, it results from a progressively intimate relationship and the loss of a separate identity.

I like how Teresa of Avila expressed it:

> During a time of conversation with Jesus, he asked her, "Who are you?"
>
> She replied, "I am Teresa of Jesus," and she asked in return, "Who are you?"
>
> And in her spirit she heard Christ say, "I am Jesus—of Teresa."[12]

More of thee and less of me. That is the goal of the Christian journey. And it happens as we open ourselves to an intimate and interactive relationship of conversation, communion, and consummation...one crumb and bubble at a time.

> The mystery that has been kept hidden for ages and generations, but is now disclosed to the saints. To them God has chosen to make known among the Gentiles the glorious riches of this mystery, which is Christ in you, the hope of glory. (Colossians 1:26-27)

~~~~~~

Bible Study: The High Priestly Prayer of Jesus

Text: John 17:13-26; Colossians 1:26-27

> I am coming to you now, but I say these things while I am still in the world, so that they may have the full measure of my joy within them. I

have given them your word and the world has hated them, for they are
not of the world any more than I am of the world. My prayer is not
that you take them out of the world but that you protect them from
the evil one. They are not of the world, even as I am not of it. Sanctify
them by the truth; your word is truth. As you sent me into the world,
I have sent them into the world. For them I sanctify myself, that they
too may be truly sanctified.

My prayer is not for them alone. I pray also for those who will
believe in me through their message, that all of them may be one,
Father, just as you are in me and I am in you. May they also be in us so
that the world may believe that you have sent me. I have given them the
glory that you gave me, that they may be one as we are one: I in them
and you in me. May they be brought to complete unity to let the world
know that you sent me and have loved them even as you have loved me.

Father, I want those you have given me to be with me where I am,
and to see my glory, the glory you have given me because you loved me
before the creation of the world.

Righteous Father, though the world does not know you, I know
you, and they know that you have sent me. I have made you known to
them, and will continue to make you known in order that the love you
have for me may be in them and that I myself may be in them.

The mystery that has been kept hidden for ages and generations, but is
now disclosed to the saints. To them God has chosen to make known
among the Gentiles the glorious riches of this mystery, which is Christ
in you, the hope of glory.

Observations

Notice three things Jesus did during his last night with his apprentices: (1) He
initiated the first communion—which became acknowledged by all Christian

bodies as the foundational sacrament of the church; (2) he encouraged his followers to remain *in* him as close as a vine and its branches; and (3) he prayed to his Father that his disciples would become one with each other and with himself and God, just as he and his Father are one.

Think of this from Jesus' perspective. Put yourself in his position. If you had one last evening to spend with your loved ones, what would you say? The most important things, of course! No more time for chitchat; no time for the nonessentials.

Jesus knew that their only prayer to survive the assaults of the enemy of their souls would be to open their hearts to his presence and power. Their only hope to overcome the world would be to live united.

The best advice Jesus had to offer his followers was to pursue union with God, and it still is.

Reflection Questions

1. What does it mean to you to be "in Christ"?
2. How does having Christ in you translate to your hope for glory?
3. How would you explain the mystery of union with God to a young child?

Meditation: Contemplative Prayer

Explanation

At one time practiced by all Christians, *lectio divina* is an ancient way of praying the Scriptures that enables the Bible, the Word of God, to become a means to union with God. It is a slow, contemplative way of allowing the Word and presence of Christ to penetrate to the center of our being and to begin a process of transforming us from the inside out.

This method of praying Scripture contains four movements. The first is called "reading" or "listening." The practice of *lectio divina* begins with cultivating the ability to listen deeply. It is a way of being more sensitive to the still, small voice of God (1 Kings 19:12); the "faint murmuring sound" that is God's Word for us, his voice touching our hearts. In *lectio* we read slowly and attentively, gently listening to hear a word or phrase that is God's communication for us this day.

The second phase of *lectio* is meditation. Through listening, we find a word, passage, or image in the Scripture that speaks to us in a personal way, then we take it in and "ruminate" on it. We ponder it in our hearts. We do this by gently repeating a keyword or phrase (or gazing on an image in the passage), allowing it to interact with our thoughts, hopes, memories, and desires. Through this phase we allow the word from God to become his word for us, a word that touches us at our deepest levels.

The third step in *lectio divina* is prayer: prayer understood as dialogue with God (that is, as loving conversation with the One who has invited us into his embrace) and as consecration (prayer as the priestly offering to God of parts of ourselves that we have not previously believed God wants). Here we allow the word we are pondering to touch and change our deepest selves.

The final phase, "contemplation," is one where there are moments when words are unnecessary. Contemplation is wordless, quiet rest in the presence of the One who loves us.[13]

Meditation

In the practice of *lectio divina* you will choose a scripture that you wish to pray. For this exercise you are asked to use the text found in the Bible study.

Here is what you do next:

1. *Place* yourself in a comfortable position and allow yourself to become silent. Allow yourself to experience the Five Ps of Prayer.

2. *Read/Listen.* Turn to the text and read it slowly, gently. Savor each portion of the reading, constantly listening for the "still, small voice" of a word or phrase that somehow says, "I am for you today."

3. *Meditate.* Next take the word or phrase into yourself. Memorize it and slowly repeat it to yourself, allowing it to interact with your inner world of concerns, memories, and ideas. Do not be afraid of distractions. Memories or thoughts are simply parts of yourself. Don't try to chase them away. Just return to the word you are pondering.

4. *Converse.* Speak to God. Whether you use words or ideas or images or all three is not important. Interact with God as you would with one who you know loves and accepts you. Give to him what you have discovered in yourself during your experience.

5. *Rest.* Finally, simply rest in God's embrace. Enjoy his presence. And when he invites you to return to your pondering of his word or to your inner dialogue with him, do so. Rejoice in the knowledge that God is with you in both words and silence.

Spiritual Exercise: Learning from a Candle

Exercise

Go back through the movements of the *lectio divina* as you focus on the flame of a candle. Consider asking God to consume all the parts of you that resist union as the flame you ponder consumes the wax and wick.

One Woman's Pursuit
of Union with God

Teresa of Avila

Union with God should be like the consummation of a marriage—the natural progression of a loving relationship in which we have taken the time for conversation and spoken with the raw honesty that leads to true communion. In union, two hearts aflame with love and desire become one. Let's look at a woman who learned to love God with her whole heart.

Teresa de Cepeda y Ahumada had a difficult name. If she had to be called to supper more than once, I assume the food got cold. She was born in Avila, Spain, in 1515 and mercifully came to be known as Teresa of Avila.

Her mother died when Teresa was fifteen. The event upset her so much that her father sent her to an Augustinian convent, where she remained for eighteen lonely months.

Three and a half years later she went to live with the Carmelite nuns at the Convent of the Incarnation. The Carmelites were supposedly a contemplative order, but the order had become quite worldly. The convent offered a life of leisure in which members had no active duties, and neither did they concentrate on contemplative prayer or enforce their separation from the outside world.[14]

For twenty years in this lukewarm climate Teresa's heart was divided between prayer and worldly interests. Then one day, at the age of thirty-nine, Teresa noticed a statue of the wounded Christ and experienced what she often referred to as a second conversion experience. The image left her vividly aware of God's presence and prompted a desire to develop a habit of constant prayer.

She began spending long hours in meditation that she called "prayer of quiet" and the "prayer of union."[15] Though never seeking mystical experiences, she did resign herself to God's will and began to experience divine encounters on a frequent basis. The most famous was a recurring vision of Christ piercing her heart with a golden spear. For Teresa this symbolized his desire for her to experience mystical union, to experience the mystery of Christ within.

Her growing intimacy with Christ was contagious. In 1562 she founded a convent in Avila with stricter rules than those in Carmelite monasteries at the time. It quickly filled, and she went on to establish many other convents. At the age of fifty-three she began to work with the twenty-six-year-old John of the Cross in reforming Carmelite monasteries. She became an important part of the internal reformation of the Catholic Church.

Teresa's relationship with God was refreshingly honest. The two had a famous exchange in 1582.

While on her way to establish her last Carmelite foundation, she and her companions encountered life-threatening flood conditions. Standing in a river torrent, she complained: "Lord, amid so many ills this comes on top of all the rest."

A voice answered her, "Teresa, that is how I treat my friends."

She retorted, "Ah, my God! That is why you have so few of them!"[16]

If this interchange really happened, it may be the only time in recorded history that someone got the last word on God. I can almost see God throwing his head back with laughter after her quip. I like to think the exchange is fact and not fiction as it reveals two important aspects of her prayer life and her movement toward union with God. First, it sounds like playful banter between friends whose relationship has become both familiar and deep. Second, it gives proper attention to the role of trials and suffering in becoming free from the world and at home with God.

In *Interior Castle,* Teresa's most famous book, she uses allegory to describe the soul's journey from outside of a castle and through many rooms as it strives toward the center room, where the soul can unite with God completely. As the soul enters and walks through the castle, it is engaged in a journey of detachment: from the world, from fears and idols, from inclination to sin, and eventually even from spiritual pleasure. It leaves behind everything that would prevent union with God.[17]

Teresa, who was blessed with many human friendships throughout her life, experienced God in the same way she enjoyed human relationships. She spent lots of time with her friends, telling experiences, sharing hopes and fears, receiving love and support, and sometimes enjoying the deepest intimacy. This is what her teaching on divine prayer is all about: taking the time to develop a friendship with the divine through deep and loving communication, and then staying with the journey until it ends in union with the one you have come to love with a whole and undivided heart. She completed the journey.

Say Yes to God's Extravagant Proposal

n early January 1974 I was sitting next to Steve, my best friend from high
school. We were waiting for class to begin with about thirty other college students. But before the biology professor could open his mouth, I got an unfor-
gettable lesson in human physiology.

A beautiful college freshman wearing a blue wool coat with flowing brown
hair, green eyes, and an armload of books entered the room and headed in our
direction. My hormones held an impromptu rodeo.

I leaned over and whispered to Steve, "I'm going to marry her." I don't
think she heard me, because she didn't seem frightened as she breezed between
us and sat down right behind me. As her perfume caught up, a thousand little
hormones hollered "Yee-ha!"

Steve did hear me. He looked at me as if I were wearing camel hair.

But time proved that my prophecy had been inspired. In less than three
years, Regina and I were married. But I'm getting ahead.

My bubbling biochemistry and fluctuating appetite told me I must be in
love. But I played it cool. I had seen a few James Bond movies and didn't want
to appear too eager. I waited until I could keep a cheeseburger down—almost
a week—before telling Regina how I felt.

She seemed very flattered but didn't do the humane thing and reciprocate
in kind. In fact, she didn't say anything. I was a prophet without honor.

After a while I found some composure, and we settled into a wonderful dating relationship. Several months and dozens of dates later, Regina said she wanted to tell me something. It was a Saturday afternoon. It comes back like yesterday. We walked inside a classroom building and sat on the steps. There was no one else around. I sat and waited. My heart was moving the buttons on my shirt. I waited. But her lips were not moving.

I stared at her mouth, hoping to see the words forming before they came out. Nothing. A period of time, something like the time needed to fight the Hundred Years' War passed. And then I heard it: "I love you."

Suddenly life made sense! My hormones were throwing confetti! My relationship with Regina reached its first crescendo that afternoon of being in her presence, waiting, and then hearing her voice.

CONVERSATION

Falling in love with Regina opened my eyes to a whole new world of shining possibilities that until that time had existed only beyond the borders of conscious awareness. Suddenly fairy tales seemed real and happily ever after became my birthright. We stepped through the doorway of self-forgetful love. And as long as we continued to treat the other as royalty, life was a kingdom.

From our first meeting, the attraction of other relationships and activities began to lessen. More than anything else in the world, I wanted to be with Regina—and fortunately, the feeling was mutual. When she wasn't around, I became preoccupied with planning ways to "accidentally" cross her path or what we might do on future dates. I was most happy only when practicing her presence.

I loved being with her and listening to her voice. My favorite times of being together involved becoming so completely still and quiet that even a Jim Croce love song was an unwanted distraction. I would sit close, listening to her voice, waiting for the words that could melt my soul, knowing with each passing syllable that the most special person in the universe loved me.

COMMUNION

Over time Regina and I discovered that we are very different. To use some familiar temperament categories: She loves being with large groups of people; I could have been a librarian—in a monastery. She is very emotional and makes decisions with her heart; Spock is my favorite Star Trek character. She's practical and down-to-earth; I live in a world of dreams and future possibilities. I'm so structured and orderly, I plan vacation itineraries a year in advance and don't think it would be a bad idea to have your canned vegetables grouped by type; she's, uh, not quite as organized as I am. I could go on, but you get the picture.

As you might expect, it wasn't too long after we were married that our cute little differences turned into sharp and grainy irritants—and there weren't any pearls being formed. As aggravation increased, we each became convinced of what needed to be done and set about re-creating the other in our own image.

At the time when our relationship should have been moving into deeper levels of communion and intimate soul sharing, resentments and rejections began to pile up and block the path to that lush garden. We became progressively more willful and more convinced it was the other who needed to change. Not only was communion a rarity, but even our conversations—which had been the sources of so much joy—frequently turned from love and acceptance to occasions for verbal assault and physical withdrawal.

For me the battle within my heart between willingness and willfulness exposed my deepest fear and most cherished idols. I was afraid to need someone without being able to control her. What if she stopped loving me? What if she changed and I could not? What if she would leave?

This fear was not new. It was a familiar feeling I had battled since the time of my earliest memories. I desperately feared abandonment and rejection and had come to use idols of perfectionism, humor, and overachievement as ways of winning acceptance. Ironically, my fear was the worst enemy to the love I craved, and my idols were barriers to true communion. I wish I could say that

I was able to lay both down when that insight slapped me on the forehead, but it wasn't that easy. I knew I needed to allow my heart to become willing, stare down my fears, and let go of my white-knuckled grip on my idols, but I was stuck.

Then, early one morning, twelve years into our marriage, I was leaving the house to go to work. Regina was standing at the front door, and I was a little surprised that she was seeing me off like June Cleaver. We had been fighting the night before. I don't remember what it was about. I don't think I knew then. She gave me a tender kiss on the cheek. Surprised again, I looked into her eyes and saw what appeared to be a deep sadness. I got into the car and backed out of the driveway and into the street.

For some reason I glanced back at the house. Regina was standing outside our front door. And even from the increasing distance, I could still see that same sad look on her face. I got an eerie feeling in my stomach.

When I returned home that night, my wife and two young daughters were gone. There was a note on the table. In the note, Regina carefully, gently, and lovingly explained that she could not live with me any longer. She wasn't divorcing me. She wasn't officially separating from me. She was simply acting on the fact that our relationship had become impossible in its present form.

I spent most of the next three weeks in tears. Exhausted and desperate, I finally became honest about my idols and how I cherished them. I placed them on the ground and walked away. Two days later my family returned. Conversation with Regina returned, and slowly, fueled by honesty and mutual humility, our relationship began to deepen into times of heart-to-heart communion.

CONSUMMATION

End of story, right? No. Surrender is never a "once and for all" experience.

Both Regina and I had to pick up our crosses and die on them each day. Some days we did. Some days we did not. Both movements into intimate communion and retreats back behind fortress walls marked the next decade. We did not become free from the grip of the past and able to move toward consummation until we both realized that hidden pockets of unforgiveness were blocking the flow of love. And we weren't able to do anything about that until we spent three days together on a prayer retreat and asked God to help us let go of the bitterness so that his love could flow freely into our hearts and back out. Forgiveness was also the key to full reconciliation.

Reconciliation has a past, present, and future. While my public commitment of devotion to Regina can be traced to a precise moment—6:23 p.m. on December 18—our love and friendship *becomes* complete as we journey together over the course of a lifetime. Reconciliation takes lavish amounts of time and honesty and an insatiable desire to remove all barriers to love. Full reconciliation requires a commitment to a journey of self-revelation and focus on the other.

Now, concerning union, I'll have to ask my mother to close the book. This part is a little embarrassing. And all I'll say to the rest of you is that there is no comparison between our honeymoon night and the intimate time we shared during the celebration of our twenty-fifth wedding anniversary. It is one thing for two people to become one; it is quite another when that happens between two people who have become fully and completely known and are still in love, much more authentically in love than when we sat together and I first waited to hear her confirming words. On our honeymoon we had sex. After twenty-five years of getting to know each other, we made love as two people fully known, two people who had finally become one, body and soul.

MANIFEST MYSTERY

I tell you the story of our romance because in many ways it parallels my relationship with God—both the positive and the negative. Just as I had to let my desire for Regina motivate me to move past my fears and abandon my idols so that we could experience heart-to-heart communion and even oneness, so my desire for Christ formation and spiritual intimacy had to lead me past a world of God-substitutes and into a lasting relationship of true closeness and familiarity with my Father.

Don't get me wrong. I still slip in and out of the stages of conversation, communion, and consummation. But each time I experience union with God, no matter how fleeting, my desire for more of God deepens—as does my belief in the basic purpose of existence. I believe we were put on earth for one reason: to learn how to fall in love with God and enjoy him forever. It's the only way a soul can become Fall-proof. It's the truest test of becoming like Jesus.

I've been in some form of relationship with God for about four decades. Initially, as a small child, I feared him and prayed that he would save me from the same fate as those flaming worms that never die, which the evangelists described. All I wanted from him was a moderate climate and the comfort of knowing I could visit with my parents for the next million years.

As a teenager, the fear phase eventually was replaced by a phase in my relationship with God where I wanted to win his recognition. Perhaps he would like me more if I would memorize large hunks of Scripture, get a perfect-attendance pin from my Sunday-school teacher, and be nice to old people. But if the truth be known, during this phase of our relationship, I was convinced that heaven was going to be more boring than a four-hour sermon delivered in a monotone.

I don't know when it happened, but all of that thinking began to change. Through reading spiritual classics, conversations with friends, and a well-timed sermon or two, I began to see God differently. I quit seeing him as a cosmic sheriff or schoolteacher. I began to see him as the prodigal's father and to believe that his love for me was not shallow and fickle, but deep and sure. And then even that image could not fully contain the love I felt he had for me. It was a love both stronger than any parent's and more romantic than any lover's.

Could it be that the Creator of the universe loved me with a reckless and boundless love, liked to hear the sound of my voice, and hung on every word? Could it be that he wanted to spend time with me and actually looked forward to my giving him my attention? Could it really be true that no matter what I did or thought, he wouldn't get angry? Was that him whispering "I understand" and "It only makes me love you more" when I confessed my sins? Could God actually be giddy with delight whenever I whispered back, "I love you"?

Yes, I have come to believe with my whole heart. God is in love with me—and each one of his prodigal children. He delights in our love for him.

Let me leave you with one of the questions that began this book. Do you ever feel that no matter how hard you try or how much you desire it, the bountiful life Jesus promised continues to elude you?

If you answered yes, then I encourage you to pursue him with the same reckless abandon with which you chased (or will chase) your spouse. Don't settle for brief encounters instead of intimate dialogue; don't become content with a salvation contract instead of enjoying communion; and don't withhold parts of your heart. Instead, pursue union. Say yes to God's extravagant proposal.

Notes

Introduction

1. See John 2; John 17; and Revelation 19:9.

Chapter 1

1. Richard J. Foster, *Prayer: Finding the Heart's True Home* (San Francisco: HarperSan-Francisco, 1992), 1-2.

2. See Luke 15:10.

3. This story is adapted from "Crumbs and Bubbles," in Garth Rosell and Stan Flewelling, eds., *The Millionaire and the Scrublady and Other Parables by William E. Barton* (Grand Rapids, Mich.: Zondervan, 1990), 59-60.

Chapter 2

1. Robert Barron, *And Now I See: A Theology of Transformation* (New York: Crossroad, 1998), 7.

2. See Matthew 6:33.

3. For a better telling of this story see Doc McConnell, "The Walkin' Catfish," in *Best-Loved Stories Told at the National Storytelling Festival: 20th Anniversary Edition* (Jonesborough, Tenn.: National Storytelling Press, 1991), 21-2.

Chapter 3

1. Carol C. Gratton, *The Art of Spiritual Guidance* (New York: Crossroad, 2000), 5.

2. St. Theophan the Recluse, quoted in Igumen Chariton of Valamo, ed., E. Kadloubovsky and E. M. Palmer, trans., *The Art of Prayer: An Orthodox Anthology* (London: Faber and Faber, 1966), 119.

3. Gray Temple, *The Molten Soul: Dangers and Opportunities in Religious Conversion* (New York: Church, 2000), 31.

4. See *The Interpreter's Dictionary of the Bible,* s.v. "Righteousness in the Old Testament."

5. A. W. Tozer, *The Pursuit of God: The Human Thirst for the Divine* (Camp Hill, Pa.: Christian Publications, 1993), 41.

6. A. W. Tozer, *The Knowledge of the Holy* (New York: Crossroad, 1992), 21.

7. Richard J. Foster and James B. Smith, eds., *Devotional Classics: Selected Readings for Individuals and Groups* (San Francisco: HarperSanFrancisco, 1993), 81.

8. Foster and Smith, *Devotional Classics,* 84.

9. Yep, this really works.

10. Henri J. Nouwen, *Out of Solitude* (Notre Dame, Ind.: Ave Maria, 1998), 14.

Chapter 4

1. See Exodus 29:43-46; Psalm 23; Isaiah 41:8; John 15:14; and Hebrews 13:5-6.

2. Quote in Richard J. Foster, *Celebration of Discipline* (San Francisco: HarperSanFrancisco, 1998), 96.

3. Peter Lord, *Hearing God* (Grand Rapids, Mich.: Baker, 1988).

4. This list was developed with Marty Goehring as part of a class lecture on practical discernment.

5. These indicators are inspired by a lecture given by Peter Lord of Titusville, Florida.

6. Frank C. Laubach, *Letters by a Modern Mystic* (Westwood, N.J.: Revell, 1937), 19.

7. Laubach, *Modern Mystic,* 17.

8. Laubach, *Modern Mystic,* 11.

9. Laubach, *Modern Mystic,* 15.

10. Laubach, *Modern Mystic,* 22.

11. Laubach, *Modern Mystic,* 26.

12. Laubach, *Modern Mystic,* 31.

13. Laubach, *Modern Mystic,* 44.

14. Frank Magill and Ian McGreal, *Christian Spirituality* (New York: Harper and Row, 1988).

Chapter 5

1. Ted M. Dorman, *A Faith for All Seasons: Historic Christian Belief in Its Classical Expressions* (Nashville: Broadman & Holman, 1995), 125.

2. See Deuteronomy 1:39 and Isaiah 7:15.

3. Dallas Willard, *Renovation of the Heart* (Colorado Springs: NavPress, 2002), 85.

4. Willard, *Renovation,* 85.

5. For a listing of the actual twelve steps, please see www.alcoholics-anonymous.org/default/en_about_aa_sub.cfm?subpageid=84&pageid=13.

Chapter 6

1. Gray Temple, *The Molten Soul: Dangers and Opportunities in Religious Conversion* (New York: Church, 2000).

2. I heard this story from Kirk Hartsfield in a restaurant. That's why he was one of my favorite teachers in college.

3. Jacob Needleman, *Money and the Meaning of Life* (New York: Doubleday, 1991), 94-6.

4. Temple, *Molten Soul,* 225.

Chapter 7

1. The dialogue between Clarence and Robert Jordan is reported by Jim McClendon and referenced in John Berman and Michael Cartwright, eds., *The Hauerwas Reader* (Durham: Duke University Press, 2001), 257-8.

2. Matthew 16:24, KJV; see also Mark 8:34 and Luke 9:23.

3. See Matthew 19:16-30; Mark 10:17-31; and Luke 18:18-30.

4. See Mark 10:21.

5. Richard J. Foster and James B. Smith, eds., *Devotional Classics: Selected Readings for Individuals and Groups* (San Francisco: HarperSanFrancisco, 1993), 33.

6. Foster and Smith, *Devotional Classics,* 34.

7. Quoted in Joyce Hollyday, "The Dream That Has Endured: Clarence Jordan and Koinonia" (on Koinonia Partners), *Sojourners,* December 1979, found at www.koinoniapartners.org/History/Overalls.

8. Thomas R. Kelly, *A Testament of Devotion* (New York: Harper & Row, 1941). This volume contains an excellent biographical memoir and lectures from Kelly.

9. Kelly, *Devotion,* 3.

10. Kelly, *Devotion,* 19.

11. Kelly, *Devotion,* 34.

12. Kelly, *Devotion,* 40.

13. Kelly, *Devotion,* 25.

14. Kelly, *Devotion,* 51.

15. Kelly, *Devotion,* 49.

16. Kelly, *Devotion,* 52, quoting Meister Eckhart to underscore the point that complete obedience is necessary if a life is to become astonishing.

17. Kelly, *Devotion,* 47.

18. Kelly, *Devotion,* 71, emphasis added.

19. Kelly, *Devotion,* 58.

20. Kelly, *Devotion,* 73.

Chapter 8

1. Lewis B. Smedes, *Forgive and Forget: Healing the Hurts We Don't Deserve* (New York: Pocket Books, 1984), 14.

2. I'm indebted to Arch Hart, a wonderful professor, who discussed the framework of this exercise during a lecture at Fuller Theological Seminary.

3. This exercise is a modified version of what is presented by Anthony de Mello in *Sadhana, A Way to God: Christian Exercises in Eastern Form* (New York: Doubleday, 1984), 75.

Chapter 9

1. F. Gregory Rogers, "Spiritual Direction in the Orthodox Tradition," *The Journal of Psychology and Theology* vol. 30, no.4 (2002): 276-89.

2. This rare burst was also inspired by a note I had jotted down while listening to a talk by Diane Langberg at a Southeast CAPS meeting in Jackson, Mississippi in 2000. My note reads, "Infinite wisdom, a little boy."

3. See Matthew 4:18-22 and John 21:1-19.

Chapter 10

1. See Genesis 34 and 1 Samuel 17:25.

2. See Rebecca Barlow Jordan, "Here Comes the Groom: Living in Joyful Anticipation of Christ's Return," *Discipleship Journal,* March/April 1995, found at www.discipleshipjournal.com/Magazines/DJ/ArticleDisplay. asp?id=110.10.

3. See Revelation 21:2 and Romans 6:5.

4. Frank C. Laubach, *Letters by a Modern Mystic* (Westwood, N.J.: Revell, 1937). See entries for May 14, 1930, and March 3, 1931.

5. See John 10:30; 14:1; and 15:1-8.

6. C. S. Lewis, *Mere Christianity* (New York: Simon & Schuster, 1980), 65.

7. See Ephesians 5:8-11.

8. This anonymous quote can be found in F. Gregory Rogers, "Spiritual Direction in the Orthodox Tradition," *Journal of Psychology and Theology* vol. 30, no. 4 (2002): 279.

9. Dallas Willard, *Renovation of the Heart* (Colorado Springs: NavPress, 2002), 38. Grateful acknowledgment is made for the use of this diagram copied from *Renovation of the Heart* by Dallas Willard, copyright 2002. Used by permission of NavPress, www.navpress.com. All rights reserved.

10. Willard, *Renovation,* 218-21.

11. Larry Crabb, *Connecting* (Nashville.: Word, 1997), xi.

12. C. L. Flinders, *Enduring Grace* (New York: Harper Collins, 1993), 190.

13. "An Introduction to the Practice of Lectio Divina," found at www.valyermo. com/ld-art.html. This article offers a helpful overview of this ancient prayer form.

14. For more information, see Alban Butler, *Butler's Lives of the Saints, Concise Edition, Revised and Updated* (San Francisco: HarperSanFrancisco, 1991).

15. Rosemary Ellen Guiley, *Harper's Encyclopedia of Mystical and Paranormal Experience* (New York: Harper Collins, 1991), 610-1.

16. See www.goodgroundpress.com/Online_Retreats/Women_Mystics/Teresa_of_ Avila/body_teresa_of_avila.

17. My favorite translation is by Kieran Kavanaugh, O.C.D., and Otilio Rodriguez, O.C.D., *Teresa of Avila: The Interior Castle* (Mahwah, N.J.: Paulist Press, 1979).

To learn more about WaterBrook Press and view
our catalog of products, log on to our Web site:
www.waterbrookpress.com

WATERBROOK
PRESS